Anonymous

The Pentucket housewife:

A manual for housekeepers, and collection of recipes

Anonymous

The Pentucket housewife:
A manual for housekeepers, and collection of recipes

ISBN/EAN: 9783337714567

Printed in Europe, USA, Canada, Australia, Japan

Cover: Foto ©ninafisch / pixelio.de

More available books at **www.hansebooks.com**

THE PENTUCKET HOUSEWIFE

A MANUAL FOR HOUSEKEEPERS,

—AND—

COLLECTION OF RECIPES.

CONTRIBUTED BY

The Ladies of the First Baptist Church

HAVERHILL, MASS.

1882.
STEAM PRESS OF CHASE BROS., 22 WASHINGTON SQUARE,
HAVERHILL, MASS.

INTRODUCTION

WITH just pride the inhabitants of Haverhill regard the name of Pentucket. In the early history of our country it had its share of "fair women and brave men," and frontier town as it was, many of these women learned to be brave as well as fair. If the name of Hannah Dustin ensures to the women of Pentucket a reputation for bravery, there were many who contributed to its renown for thrift and hospitality.

A genial social intercourse distinguished the older families, and at their frequent gatherings, abundance and excellence characterized the provisions of the table.

These ancient dames were competent to discuss with wisdom the complicated affairs of colonial and revolutionary times, and equally able to organize the household, control the children, and direct the servants; especially able to do the last because they were personally familiar with the details of domestic life. Cooking, washing, brewing and even soap-making were reckoned among their accomplishments.

It is believed that a good share of ability and thrift has descended to their children, and that even in these degenerate days, we may justly boast of many "capable women." It is also found that the ladies of the present day, like their grandmothers, are fond of discussing comparative methods of housekeeping, and many a choice recipe is passed from one to another over tables adorned with most delicate of biscuit and cakes, and fragrant with aroma of coffee and tea.

Under the impression that it is wise to gather up some of these excellent recipes and give them the permanence secured by a book, the present work has been undertaken; and it is hoped that the historical interest of the older rules, the excellence of the modern ones, with the guarantee given to the most of them by the reliable names appended, will make our collection of special interest to ourselves and of real value to others.

In the faith that it will tend to perpetuate the superior housekeeping of our honored mothers, and make those who shall come after us worthy representatives of the dear ones who have gone before, it is respectfully dedicated to those who now have the honor to be the matrons of Haverhill and vicinity.

HAVERHILL, MASS., Dec., 1882.

"She seeketh wool and flax, and worketh willingly with her hands."

"She riseth early while it is yet night, and giveth meat to her household."

"She looketh well to the ways of her household, and eateth not the bread of idleness."

SOLOMON.

What does cookery mean? It means the knowledge of all fruits and herbs and balms and spices, and of all that is healing and sweet in fields and groves, and savory in meats. It means carefulness and inventiveness, and watchfulness and willingness, and readiness of appliance. It means the economy of your great-mother and the science of modern chemists. It means much tasting and no wasting; it means English thoroughness, and French art, and Arabian hospitality; and it means, in fine, that you are to be perfectly and always ladies—loaf givers; and as you are to see imperatively that everybody has something pretty to put on, so you are to see even yet more imperatively that everybody has something nice to eat.

RUSKIN.

"Pease porridge hot,
Pease porridge cold,
Pease porridge in the pot
Nine days old."

STOCK.

Buy a shank of beef and have it broken into small pieces; put with it any bones or fragments you may have of cooked or uncooked meat. Allow about a quart of cold water, a teaspoonful of salt and a little pepper to each pound of meat. Put over the fire and let it come to boil slowly, skimming off every particle of skum as it rises. A little cold water added just as it boils will make the skum rise more freely. After this, cover closely and let it boil very slowly for several hours. Strain out all the meat and bones, which, having parted with all their juices, are good for nothing, and keep the broth to use as may be needed. When ready to use it, remove the cake of fat which has formed on the top, and save it for shortening, or for the fry-kettle. If the stock is to be used immediately, vegetables may be used as well as meat, but not if the stock is to be kept any time, as vegetable juices very soon ferment. Stock thus prepared is useful for all kinds of soups, gravies and hashes.

MOCK TURTLE SOUP.

To about one gallon of good beef stock put one coffee cupful of black beans, soaked in cold water over night. Let them boil till they are soft enough to mash easily; skim out the beans, mash very perfectly, put back into the soup kettle; mix well and strain the whole through a strainer fine enough to retain all the hulls from the beans. Return to the soup kettle, add salt, a very little red pepper, two teaspoonfuls of flour. Boil for a few minutes. Slice a nice fresh lemon into your tureen and pour upon it the soup.—*Mrs. J. C. Tyler*, Boston.

MRS. VINTON'S SOUP.

Take the scraps and bones of cold roast beef, mutton or the skeleton of a roast turkey, to which add a small joint of beef or veal. Boil until the meat cleaves from the bones. Strain out the bones and meat, return the meat to the broth and let it stand over night in a cool place. Take off the fat and put the broth back into the soup kettle. Cut into dice shaped pieces, half a turnip, half a carrot, a stick of celery and two potatoes; add them to the soup and let all boil slowly an hour and a half. When the soup is put on to cook, put half a cupful of pearl barley to soak on the back of the range and add it to the soup half an hour before serving. Take a small piece of light dough, or make up a little biscuit dough, and cut a dozen small dumplings with a pepper box cover and drop them into the soup fifteen minutes before serving.—*Julia A. Marshall, M. D.*

CORN SOUP.

Grate a dozen ears of corn. Boil the cobs twenty minutes, putting them on in cold water. Remove the cobs, and boil the grated corn twenty minutes in the same water. Then add a pint of milk, a little butter, pepper, salt, and water enough to make the soup just right for thickness. Just before serving remove the soup from the fire, add two or three well beaten eggs and send at once to the table.—*Mrs. Merrihen*, Fairhaven.

GREEN PEA SOUP.

Boil one quart of green pease and one onion until the pease are very tender. Mash, and add a pint of stock, two tablespoonfuls of butter and one of flour rubbed together. Boil and add two cupfuls of rich milk. Season, strain and serve. Bread spread with butter, cut into squares and toasted in the oven, makes a nice addition to the soup.—*S. P.*

BEAN SOUP.

One pound of the round of beef, one-half pound of salt pork, one quart of black beans, a few stalks of celery and an onion. Soak the beans over night. Chop the beef and pork. Simmer all together for five or six hours. Strain and season to taste. Serve with lemons, sliced. Excellent pea or bean soup can be made by boiling the beans or pease with celery and onions in corned-beef liquor, if it be not too salt.—*Miss Carrie Duncan.*

LOBSTER SOUP—No. 1.

One large lobster or two small ones; pick all the meat from the shell and chop fine; scald one quart of milk and one pint of water, then add the lobster, a lump of butter, a tablespoonful of flour, salt and red pepper to taste. Boil ten minutes and serve hot.—*Miss Rebecca W. Duncan.*

LOBSTER SOUP—No. 2.

To one lobster, chopped, add three pounded crackers mixed with the green of the lobster and a piece of butter the size of an egg. Scald one quart of milk; as soon as it comes to boil stir in the ingredients. Season with pepper.—*Miss A. E. Goodrich.*

TOMATO SOUP—No. 1.

One can of tomatoes stewed and strained; add a pinch of soda. Boil three quarts of milk and thicken it with a tablespoonful of corn starch wet in a little cold milk. Add butter size of an egg, salt and pepper. Pour the tomato into the milk and serve hot.—*Mrs. Marianne Ely.*

TOMATO SOUP—No. 2.

One quart of canned tomatoes, one pint of hot water, onions—more or less; let them come to boil; two heaping tablespoonfuls of flour, one tablespoonful of butter, one teaspoonful of sugar, one teaspoonful of salt, well rubbed together with a spoonful of the hot tomato. When very smooth, stir into the boiling mixture; boil fifteen minutes, add pepper and rub through a sieve. Serve with squares of toasted bread.—*Mrs. Dr. S. K. Towle.*

TOMATO SOUP—No. 3.

Take pieces of roast beef or beefsteak that cannot be used in any other way; boil them slowly several hours. Set this away until cold, so that all the fat can be removed, then add salt, onions cut fine, one quart tomatoes, pepper, and a tablespoonful of ground cloves. Boil all together until the meat is all in shreds; strain and thicken; return to the fire and boil three or four minutes.—*A. T. B.*

PARKER HOUSE TOMATO SOUP.

Five pints of beef liquor, two onions, one carrot, one turnip, one beet. Pare them and cut in small pieces, boil forty-five minutes and strain through a sieve; add two quarts of tomatoes; boil twenty minutes and strain. Brown a quarter of a pound of butter, or less; stir in flour until it makes a paste; pour into the soup and boil ten minutes; add a teaspoonful of sugar and salt to taste.

POTATO SOUP.

Ten large potatoes boiled soft and mashed with one-quarter of a pound of butter. Pour on three pints of boiling milk, and stir all the time until it boils again. Season with salt, pepper and mace. Strain into the tureen, and serve with squares of fried bread.—*Mrs. T. G. Appleton.*

BEAN PORRIDGE.

Boil four pounds of corned beef and one pint of white pea beans in four quarts of water for two hours, (skimming thoroughly,) then add one pound of fat pork and boil two hours more; add water to have four quarts when done. Take out the meat and pork, mix one pint of sifted Indian meal in cold water and pour into the liquor. Stir well and let it boil five minutes.—*Mrs. J. F. Gile.*

FORCE MEAT BALLS FOR SOUP.

Take any kind of cold meat; chop very fine; add an egg and bread crumbs or flour; season well with pepper and salt. Make up into small balls and fry them brown.—*T. W. C.*

NOODLES FOR SOUP.

To one egg add as much sifted flour as it will absorb, with a little salt; roll out as thin as a wafer, dredge lightly with flour, roll over and over into a large roll, slice from the ends and drop into the soup about five minutes before serving.

DUMPLINGS FOR SOUP.

A pint of flour and a little salt, a teaspoonful of cream of tartar and half as much soda; mix with milk a little softer than for biscuit; drop from a spoon into the boiling soup; take them out of the soup as soon as they are cooked, as they become heavy by remaining in it.

FISH.

"It is observable, not only that there are fish three times as big as the mighty elephant, but that the mightiest feasts have been of fish. The Romans, in the hight of their glory, have made fish the mistress of all their entertainments."—IZAAK WALTON.

TO BAKE A BLUEFISH.

Take a bluefish weighing three or four pounds, rub into it a dessert spoonful of salt, one-half teaspoonful each of sage and summer savory. Make a dressing of two pounded crackers, one egg well beaten, a little salt and pepper, and two tablespoonfuls of milk or water. Lay the fish on a tin sheet that will fit loosely into the baking pan. Gash the fish on top, leaving an inch space between the gashes; put a thin strip of salt pork in the gashes, and on the spaces lay a small roll of the dressing. Turn into the baking pan half a cup of water, (not more, or the fish will boil instead of bake), adding more water if it boils away. Bake one hour, then lift out the fish on the tin sheet, place the pan on the fire, and when the gravy boils, thicken with one teaspoonful of flour, and season with salt and pepper. Slip the fish off the tin sheet into a platter and pour the gravy around it.—*Mrs. C. B. Emerson.*

BAKED HALIBUT,

Upon the grate of the dripping pan put a buttered sheet of thick white writing paper; place the lump of fish upon the paper; cover the top with powdered cracker, salt and bits of butter. Bake in a hot oven until well browned—about an hour for two pounds. Slip from the paper on to the platter; garnish with slices of hard-boiled egg; serve with butter sauce.—*Mrs. Leonard Whittier.*

BAKED SHAD.

Have the shad opened in the back, with the head left on; stuff, sew together, and place in the dripping pan with a little water; lay over it two or three thin slices of pork, dredge with flour and bake one hour in a hot oven; baste two or three times. After it has been baking one half-hour, add a little butter; about ten minutes before it is done, add one-half cup of milk and a little flour.—*Mrs. Freeman Q. Barrows.*

BAKED FISH.

After the fish is cleaned, rub it with salt and fill it with a highly-seasoned force-meat. Sew it up, put the tail in the mouth, strew it with powdered cracker, sweet herbs, cloves, and small bits of butter. Put a pint of water in the pan. Most fishes need to bake about two hours. When half done, baste with butter. Pour the gravy off into a sauce-pan, add browned flour, pepper and cloves, until it is highly seasoned. Garnish the dish with lemon and balls of the force meat.—*Mrs. J. H. Duncan.*

CREAM FISH.

Boil two pounds of cod or halibut, and break into small pieces while hot. Add a few small pieces of butter, a little pepper and salt. Make a sauce with one pint of milk in which has been boiled a small onion, one-fourth of a pound of butter, and thickened with two tablespoonfuls of flour; let it boil to thicken. Cover the bottom of a dish with the fish, add some sauce, and so on, fish and sauce, until the dish is filled. Cover the top with breadcrumbs, bits of butter and the juice of one lemon. Brown in the oven.—*Mrs. H. C. Graves.*

TURBOT A LA CREME.

Take five pounds of boiled fish, shred the fish while hot, then set away to cool. Boil one quart of milk and in it one-quarter of an onion, a little piece of parsley and a scant cup of flour mixed with a part of the milk while cold. Boil this till it thickens a little, take out the onion and parsely and turn the milk upon two beaten yolks of eggs. Season it with two teaspoonfuls of salt, half a teaspoonful of thyme, quarter of a teaspoonful of pepper, and half a cup of butter. Then butter a pudding-dish and put in alternate layers of fish and cream, finishing with cream. Sift over the top cracker dust and grated cheese, and bake half an hour.—*Mrs. E. N. Hill.*

BAKED SALT FISH.

Soak one-half pound of salt codfish in warm water over night. Spread on the bottom of a quart dish a piece of butter the size of an egg. Put in the fish shredded fine, one and a half cracker, pounded, a little pepper, one beaten egg, two cups of scalded milk. Bake twenty-five minutes. Very nice with baked potatoes.—*Mrs. Susan Kimball.*

SHAKER CODFISH.

Soak half a pound of salt fish, and cook it slightly. Boil four or five potatoes and cut into thick slices. Boil three eggs just hard enough to slice. Make a rich white sauce with milk and butter, thickened with a little flour. Put the ingredients together over the fire, add pepper and serve very hot. — *Mrs. John Lincoln,* Providence.

FISH BALLS.

Soak the fish over night. In the morning change the water, and after a little more soaking put it into tepid water, cover close and put it where it will be very hot, but on no account let it boil, as this makes it hard and unpalatable. After being cooked in this way for an hour or two it is ready for fish balls or any other use. For fish balls, chop very fine, add twice the quantity of mashed potatoes, moisten with butter or rich cream, add pepper, or mustard, if you like, and a little salt if the fish does not salt it sufficiently. Mix all very thoroughly. Make into little flat cakes, flour, and fry in the spider, in the fat of fried pork, which is to be served with them; or, make into round balls, egg and crumb them, and fry in boiling lard.

RAW OYSTERS

Drain them in a colander, sprinkle with plenty of pepper and salt, and put them on ice at least half an hour before serving; or they may be placed upon the table in a block of ice.

FRICASSEE OF OYSTERS.

Scald one quart of oysters in their liquor, then strain off the liquor. Put a piece of butter the size of an egg into a saucepan on the stove, and when it bubbles sprinkle in a tablespoonful of flour; let it cook a minute, stirring it, then add the liquor. Take it from the fire and add the yolks of two eggs, salt and a little pepper. Return it to the fire and put in the oysters; boil all together a minute and serve on toasted bread, or crackers split and toasted.—*Mrs. J. A. Hale.*

OYSTER STEW.

Three pints of milk. When it boils, stir in two tablespoonfuls of cracker dust, salt and two tablespoonfuls of butter; add one quart of oysters and let them just reach the boiling point.—*Mrs. Luther Day.*

FRIED OYSTERS.

Sprinkle the oysters with pepper and salt, and cool thoroughly before cooking. When ready to cook, roll them first in cracker crumbs, then in egg, or egg and milk, then in cracker crumbs again. Fry in boiling lard, like doughnuts, or in butter in a hot spider, and serve immediately.

ESCALOPED OYSTERS—No. 1.

One quart of oysters, one pint of fine cracker crumbs, one pint of milk, one egg, butter, salt and pepper. First put a layer of oysters and season well with salt, pepper and butter, then cover with a layer of the cracker crumbs, and repeat till the oysters are all used, and also the liquor. Have the top layer of crumbs. Beat the egg thoroughly, stir it into the milk and pour over the top of the dish, which must be large enough to allow for the swelling.—*Mrs. E. G. Wood.*

ESCALOPED OYSTERS—No. 2.

For one quart of oysters take five or six Boston crackers finely powdered. Butter the dish and add a sprinkling of cracker crumbs then a layer of oysters; add seasoning of salt and pepper; cover with crumbs and place on them small bits of butter. Fill the dish in this manner, having three layers of the oysters and ending with the cracker crumbs. Put a goodly number of bits of butter on the last crumbs, and bake in a hot oven about half an hour. Do not use any of the liquor with the oysters, except what will remain after dipping them out with the fork.—*Mrs. E. W. Ames.*

CLAM CHOWDER.

One quart of clams, one quart of sliced potatoes. Make six alternate layers of potatoes and clams. Sprinkle a little pepper and salt pork fat over each layer of clams. Cover completely with boiling water, and boil about twenty minutes, or until the potato is done. While this is boiling, soak about eighteen crackers in two quarts of milk, and add to the chowder when the potato is done. Salt, if necessary. Let it just boil after adding the crackers.—*Mrs. Newton Stover.*

LOBSTER CHOPS.

Cut one-half pound of the meat of lobster into small bits. Mix smooth in a stew-pan a piece of butter about the size of half an egg, and a tablespoonful of flour; add two-thirds of a cupful of milk or cream, and when it boils stir in the lobster; then take it from the fire and add two beaten eggs, cayenne pepper and salt to the taste; return the mixture to the fire and stir until the eggs are set. When cold, form the mixture into the shape of chops, pointed at one end. Roll in bread crumbs, then in egg, and again in the crumbs, and fry in hot butter.—*Mrs. Moses Giddings*, Bangor, Me.

MEAT.

"We may live without poetry, music and art;
We may live without conscience, and live without heart;
We may live without friends, and live without books;.
But civilized man cannot live without cooks.
He may live without books—what is knowledge but grieving?
He may live without hope—what is hope but deceiving?
He may live without love—what is passion but pining?
But where is the man that can live without dining."

---※---

To boil meat for the table, put it into boiling water. The albumen of the meat is thus hardened at the surface, and a case is formed to retain the juices. Boil steadily but very gently, as hard boiling toughens the meat. If to be eaten cold, allow it to cool in the water in which it was boiled, thereby greatly improving the flavor.

To roast meat, place it upon bars in the dripping pan, flour it well, put a little water into the pan, add more when this is nearly dried away. Baste the meat often in its own juice, or butter, if you please. When half done turn over to brown the other side. Some persons rub salt over the meat before flouring it for the oven, others, thinking this method causes a waste of the juices, prefer to salt a half hour before serving. A little boiling water thrown upon beef just before it goes into the oven will tend to retain the juices and secure rare roasting.

Beef should have a very hot oven from the first; poultry, pork and lamb, a more moderate oven to begin with.

To make the gravy, take up the meat upon a hot platter, and keep it in a hot place. Dip or pour off all the fat from the dripping pan, then put the pan upon the top of the stove; add boiling water if you have not enough in the pan; thicken with browned flour, wet in cold water; stir and boil all together until quite smooth; add salt if it is needed, and strain for the table.

To broil steaks, have a clear fire of well-burnt coals. Use either a broiler or toaster, but the latter is the more convenient. Turn as often as the meat begins to drip. Do not salt until it is done, as salt tends to draw out the juices. Add pepper and bits of butter and serve immediately upon a hot platter.

STEAMED TURKEY.

Rub pepper and salt inside the turkey. Fill the body with oysters and sew it up carefully. Cover closely in the steamer, and steam from two to three hours; then take it up; strain the gravy which will be found in the dish; have an oyster sauce ready, prepared like stewed oysters, and pour this gravy, thickened with a little butter and flour, into the oyster sauce. Let it just boil, and add a little boiled cream. Pour the sauce over the turkey and serve immediately.—*T.*

JELLIED TURKEY.

Cut the turkey into pieces of convenient size to pack nicely into the kettle, and cover with cold water to three times the depth of the meat. Add salt, and bring slowly to the boiling point, skimming thoroughly before boiling. Continue to cook slowly until the meat falls from the bones. The liquor should be boiled down to a quantity just to cover all. During the last of the boiling, it should be seasoned to taste, with salt, pepper, and celery salt, if desired. Separate all the nice meat from the bones, placing it in a dish or mould—a bread pan being a good shape to slice from. If the meat is laid length-wise of the mould it will be nicer when sliced. Strain the liquor upon the meat, and when cold place on ice to harden. The only difficulty in preparing this dish is in the quantity to which the liquor is reduced. It would better be reduced too much than not enough.—*Mrs. Geo. W. Bosworth.*

BONED CHICKEN.

Boil the chicken in as little water as possible, until tender enough to slip from the bones easily, then chop a little, put back in the water, season to taste with salt, pepper and butter, place over the fire and cook a little more, then put into molds. The yolks of two or three eggs, stirred in when cooking the last time, will improve the dish.—*Mrs. H. S. Littlefield.*

PRESSED CHICKEN.

Boil one chicken very tender and shred it. Boil three eggs hard. Put one egg cut in two parts lengthwise in the bottom of a quart mold, with half a small pickle, each half of the egg placed face down; then put in the meat, filling eggs and pickles on the sides and ends, the same as the bottom. Season the liquor with salt and pepper, boil it down, and pour over the whole. Set in a cool place. As it cools, the meat will jelly so as to pour out nicely.—*Mrs. H. S. Littlefield.*

CHICKEN FRICASSEE.

Take a boiled chicken cut suitably to serve, fry it in butter and remove to a hot dish. Take the liquor in which the chicken was boiled, and when boiling add to it one egg mixed with two tablespoonfuls of brown flour and a little milk. Season with salt, pepper, and chopped parsley. Pour the gravy over the chicken. A few slices of onion, fried in the butter, improve it for some persons.—*Mrs. Luther Day.*

CHICKEN CURRY WITH RICE.

Cut one-third of a pound of salt pork in slices and fry crisp. In this fat fry quite brown two large onions cut thin; add one and a half pint of rich chicken broth, and one and a half pound of cold chicken cut in small bits. Grate one half cup of fresh cocoanut. Pound in a mortar the rest of the cocoanut; squeeze in one cup of water to get out as much milk as possible. Add this milk to the grated cocoanut, and put into the frying-pan. Mix three tablespoonfuls of India curry powder and one tablespoonful of corn starch in a little cold broth; add to this mixture, with the juice of two lemons and a little of the grated rind, a piece of butter as large as an egg; let it simmer three hours. If it boils away much, add a little hot water.

TO COOK THE RICE.

Put two cups of rice in six quarts of boiling water, let it boil very fast fifteen minutes, then put in two heaping tablespoonfuls of salt and boil five minutes more, turn into a colander and drain dry. The curry is served as a gravy on the rice. Veal, beef and liver may be used instead of chicken, in the same way.—*Miss Katie Fairbank,* Ahmednagah, India.

CHICKEN WITH WHITE SAUCE—No. 1.

Take the white meat of one chicken, boiled or roasted; cut it the size of almonds. Mix a quarter of a pound of butter and one tablespoonful of flour together; add a pint of boiling milk; after mixing put on the fire. When again boiling, add chicken and two or three hard-boiled eggs chopped fine; let it all simmer a few minutes; season with red pepper and salt.—*Mrs. J. Houston West.*

CHICKEN WITH WHITE SAUCE—No. 2.

Boil the chicken whole; salt the water enough to season it well just before it is done. Boil a quart of milk; stir into it one egg, a piece of butter the size of an egg, a little salt, and corn starch enough to thicken. Put the chicken on the platter and pour the sauce over it.—*Mrs. E. H. Drew.*

POTTED PIGEONS.

Stuff the pigeons as for a roast. Try out a few slices of pork, and brown the pigeons; brown also a few slices of onion. Cover the pigeons with water, putting in salt, pepper, and a little pounded clove; stew until tender. Serve on crackers in a deep dish. Add dumplings, if you choose.—*Mrs. C. S. Emmerton*, Peabody.

MOCK DUCK.

Take a nice tender round steak; make stuffing as for turkey; spread the stuffing on the steak; roll it up and tie it. Roast from half to three-quarters of an hour, basting with butter.—*Mrs. C. W. Train.*

ROAST HAM.

Put the ham in a roasting pan with a little water, and let it roast for about two hours, then take off the skin and put the ham back into the oven. A medium-sized ham will require from four to five hours. When taken from the oven, sprinkle with bread crumbs, and garnish with cloves, if desired.—*Mrs. Geo. W. Duncan.*

TO BOIL CORNED BEEF.

Select a piece that has been not too long in the brine. Put it into hot water and watch it, to skim as it begins to boil. Then cover it closely and set it where it will keep at the boiling point for four or five hours, according to size. Hard boiling will make it tough. When very tender, set it away in the covered kettle until cold, then take it out and press it. If you wish to eat a part of it hot, cut off what may be needed and return the rest to cool in the water in which it was boiled, as this greatly enriches it.—*Mrs. C. W. Train.*

SPICED PRESSED BEEF.

Boil a shin of beef having on it four pounds of lean meat and gristle, with four bird peppers, five hours in water enough to cover it; then let the water simmer till a pint remains. Take out the bones, chop the meat and gristle a little, mix with the juice, and season with one tablespoonful of salt, one teaspoonful each of sage and summer savory, one and a half teaspoonful of curry powder, one-fourth teaspoonful each of clove, pimento and pepper; add two pounded crackers, put in a deep dish, cover with a plate and press down with a weight. Cut in thin slices when cold.—*Mrs. Susan Kimball.*

CANNELON OF BEEF.

Two pounds of beef, rind of half a lemon, three sprigs of parsley, teaspoonful of salt, quarter of a teaspoonful of pepper, two tablespoonfuls of melted butter, one raw egg. Chop meat, parsley and lemon rind very fine; shape into a roll, bake on buttered paper about thirty minutes, and serve with tomato sauce.

STEWED BEEF.

Buy the middle cut of the rump. For ten pounds, add five quarts of water and cook six hours. Put into the water, a bunch of pot herbs, a head of celery, two small onions—each stuck with two cloves, one large carrot, two small turnips cut fine, one pepper, a little salt. This makes a strong gravy, to be served with and around the meat. It is better to cut the carrot and cook until tender, scald the onions separately, and put in with the meat. The turnips may be scalded, fried, and served around the dish. It must never boil, but simmer slowly on the back of the range.—*Mrs. J. B. Swett.*

GULASH (Hungarian Dish.)

Proportions: To two pounds beef without fat, a soup plate of fine cut onions, butter enough to brown them, as much potato as meat, and as much red pepper as can be taken up on the point of a knife. Use a kettle with a close-fitting cover, as the meat is to be cooked in its own juice. Put the onions and butter in a kettle over a hot fire and stir till browned. Then put in the meat cut in small pieces, with the salt and pepper. Cook slowly, without stirring, till tender, adding a little water, if necessary. With two pounds of meat, water must be added, as there will not be gravy enough from it. The more meat there is used, the less need there will be of water. Requires usually three or four hours' cooking. Put the potatoes, cut in dice, on the top an hour before taking up. Serve hot.—*Mrs. E. G. Wood.*

BAKED CALVES' LIVER.

Lard the liver with fat pork, and put it into an iron pan with a pint of water or stock. Bake it three-fourths of an hour, basting it very often. Dish the liver. Add to the gravy a piece of butter the size of an egg, a little flour, pepper and salt. Boil once and pour over the liver.—*Mrs. A. Robeson*, Brookline.

SWEET-BREAD.

Sweet-breads should be eaten very fresh or not at all. Soak them in cold water for about an hour, then boil them in salted boiling water or stock until tender—about twenty minutes. When ready to serve, sprinkle with pepper and salt, roll them in egg and bread crumbs and fry in hot lard or butter.—*Mrs. M. Giddings*, Bangor, Me.

SAUSAGE MEAT.

Twelve pounds of minced meat, one small teacup of salt, two large tablespoonfuls of sage, one tablespoonful of pepper, one large tablespoonful of summer savory.—*Mrs. J. K. Smith.*

BREAST OF VEAL.

Take a breast of veal, omitting the shoulder. Make a stuffing as for turkey and put it under the bones wherever you can, holding it in place with skewers. Put it in a kettle with just water enough to cover it. Simmer about two hours. Lay on thin slices of salt pork; dredge with flour; put into a dripping pan with some of the liquor in which it was boiled; roast for an hour, until well browned. Make balls of some of the force meat; fry them and use with sliced lemon to garnish the dish. Use the remaining liquor, with that in the pan, for the gravy.—*Mrs. J. H. Duncan.*

VEAL LOAF.

Three pounds of veal and half a pound of salt pork chopped very fine; two eggs well beaten; one teacupful of powdered cracker, four teaspoonfuls of salt, three teaspoonfuls of black pepper, (if you please, one of clove.) Knead well together and bake an hour and a half in a well-buttered pan. To be eaten cold.—*Mrs. L. Whittier.*

JELLIED VEAL.

A knuckle of veal. Boil slowly till the meat slips easily from the bones; take out of the liquor; remove the bones; chop the meat fine; season with salt, pepper, mace, sage and thyme. Put back into the liquor and boil until it is almost dry, and stirs with difficulty; turn into a mold and set away until cold. The juice of lemon, added just before taking from the fire, is a great improvement.—*Mrs. J. Houston West.*

CHOPS, AND TOMATO SAUCE.

Steam the chops three quarters of an hour, or until very tender. Mince some bread very fine; beat an egg very light; dip the chops into the egg, then roll in bread crumbs and fry a delicate brown.

SAUCE.

Stew six tomatoes half an hour, with two cloves, a little parsley, pepper and salt. Put a little butter into a hot sauce-pan, and when it bubbles stir into it a heaping teaspoonful of flour; mix and cook it well, and add the cooked tomato; stir until thoroughly smooth. Arrange the chops on a platter and pour the sauce around them.—*Mrs. A. H. Strong,* Rochester, N. Y.

SALT PORK IN BATTER.

Cut one-half pound of salt pork in slices one-fourth of an inch thick; cut off the rind and pour over them boiling water, in which let them stand five minutes; turn off the water and fry till they are cooked on both sides. Make a batter of one-third of a cup of milk, one well-beaten egg, a little salt, one-fourth of a teaspoonful of cream of tartar, one eighth of a teaspoonful of soda, and five tablespoonfuls of flour. Dip the pieces of cooked pork into this batter and fry in pork fat like fritters.—*Mrs. Susan Kimball.*

FRAGMENTS.

"Though on pleasure she was bent,
She had a frugal mind."
COWPER.

REMNANTS OF BEEF.

Take all the remnants of roast beef—bones, bits of meat and gravy, excluding all fat; cover with cold water and simmmer on the back of the stove until the meat falls from the bones. Skim out the meat and put in some canned or fresh tomatoes; stew until the tomatoes are cooked; strain, thicken and season; put back the bits of meat; boil up once; add squares of toasted bread and send to the table.—*Mrs. M. Giddings*, Bangor.

REMNANTS OF BEEF—No. 2.

Take cold roast beef, or roast meat of any kind, slice it thin, cut it rather small, and lay it, wet with gravy and sufficiently peppered and salted, in a meat-pie dish. If liked, a small onion may be chopped fine and sprinkled over it. Over the meat pour a couple of stewed tomatoes, a little more pepper, and a thick layer of mashed potatoes. Bake slowly in a moderate oven till the top is a light brown.—*H. H. T.*

CHOWDER OF REMNANTS.

Trim off all fat or gristle from cold roast beef, beefsteak, or any kind of meat, and cut into small bits. Add a few sliced potatoes, a sliced onion, salt, pepper, and any gravy which may have been left from meat, cover all with water and cook until the potatoes are done.

REMNANTS OF FISH.

Use any kind of fresh fish. Shred it fine. Cover with it the bottom of a deep dish well buttered; sprinkle over cracker crumbs, salt, pepper, and bits of butter; repeat until the dish is filled, having crumbs on top. Moisten with milk, and bake until brown.

MINCED MUTTON.

Mince the cold mutton, season well, and add a cup of good gravy, warmed and strained. Strew the bottom of a dish with dry crumbs, pour the mixture upon it, cover with fine crumbs and set in the oven till very hot; then break eggs enough over the top to cover the mixture well, inserting bits of butter here and there; pepper and salt; sift pounded cracker lightly upon the eggs, and return to the oven until they are set.

MEAT PATTIES.

Line small patty pans with good puff paste and bake in a quick oven. Chop remnants of chicken, or other meat, fine; season with salt and pepper, and heat in a little butter sauce. Fill the shells and put them back into the oven till the mixture is slightly browned. A little flavoring of tomato improves some meats used in this way.—*Mrs. M. Giddings*, Bangor, Me.

MOULD OF MEAT.

Take as much cold meat of any kind as you may require for the size of your mould; mince it very fine. Soak a small quantity of bread crumbs in any stock, if you have it, if not, in milk;

mix this with the meat, then add salt, pepper, ketchup, and an egg, well beaten, to bind it all together. Butter a plain tin mould, dredge it with flour, fill it with the mixture, flour over the top, tie a cloth over it and boil for an hour. When done, turn it out of the mould and serve with a thick brown gravy over it.— *Mrs. A. Robeson*, Brookline.

REMNANTS OF PORK.

Bits of cold roast pork may be chopped very fine, seasoned with salt and pepper, moistened (if need be) with a little water, and baked in paste as turnovers.—*C. M.*

CORNED BEEF HASH.

Chop cold corned beef fine; mash potatoes and add to them a piece of butter the size of an egg; chop sour apples and mix with the potato and meat in equal quantities. Put the mixture in a pan with a little butter and let it stand in a moderate oven three-quarters of an hour, or a little longer, according to the quantity made.—*Miss A. G. Beckwith.*

HAM RELISH.

Take pieces (no matter how small) of cold ham, chop fine, season with mustard, pepper, and salt if necessary, moisten with a beaten egg and a little cream or milk. Heat through and put in a glass or jar to cool. A nice relish for tea, or for sandwiches. Will keep several days.—*Mrs. A. L. George.*

DEVILED HAM.

Use any odds and ends of cooked ham, but see that at least a quarter of the amount is fat. Chop very fine—almost to a paste. For a pint of this make a dressing as follows: One even tablespoonful of sugar, one even tablespoonful of mustard, a little cayenne pepper, one teacupful of vinegar. Mix the sugar, mustard and pepper thoroughly, and add the vinegar little by little. Stir it into the chopped ham, and pack it in small molds. Serve upon a small platter and garnish with parsley; or it may be spread between slices of buttered bread for sandwiches.

CROQUETTES.

One pint of any kind of cold meat, (if of several kinds, the better,) chopped very fine; one teaspoonful of salt, one-fourth of a teaspoonful of cayenne, one sprig of chopped parsley, one egg. Mix all together and moisten with milk or cream sufficiently to form in the hands. When shaped, dip them into beaten egg and then in powdered bread crumbs, into which pepper and salt have been shaken, and fry in boiling lard for a minute and a half. The fat should be hot enough to brown a piece of bread while you count forty.—*Mrs. A. Robeson*, Brookline.

CHICKEN CROQUETTES.

Chop a little, the meat of a good-sized chicken from which bones, fat and skin have been removed. Season with salt and pepper. Place in a saucepan on the range a piece of butter the size of an egg; when melted add a small half cup of flour and stir constantly; when well mixed, add enough of the water in which the chicken was boiled to make the sauce the consistency of thick cream; then add the chopped meat, just let it heat through, and fry as croquettes.—*Miss Train*, Newton Centre.

POTATO CROQUETTES.

Season cold mashed potatoes with pepper, salt and nutmeg; beat to a cream, with a tablespoonful of melted butter to every cupful of potato; add two or three beaten eggs and some minced parsley. Roll into small balls, dip in beaten egg, then in cracker crumbs, and fry in hot lard. Cold boiled rice may be used in place of potatoes.—*Mrs. Dr. O. D. Cheney.*

EGGS

"The vulgar boil, the learned roast an egg."—POPE.

SCRAMBLED EGGS.

Put the eggs in a moderately heated pan, add butter, salt and pepper, and milk, if you please; stir constantly until the eggs thicken.

POACHED EGGS.

Have the frying-pan full of salted water, just gently boiling. Break each egg into a cup and slide into the water. Let them stand without boiling for five minutes. Take them up on a skimmer, and slip on to slices of toast, moistened with hot water and butter. Serve immediately.

BAKED EGGS.

Break the eggs into a buttered pudding dish, sprinkle over salt and pepper, and bake in a quick oven, until set. Serve in the same dish.

OMELET—No. 1.

Eight eggs; separate the whites from the yolks; beat the whites till they will stand alone; beat the yolks with two tablespoonfuls of cornstarch or flour, a little pepper, salt, and one cup of milk. Mix all with the whites very lightly. Have the pan hot; use butter the size of a walnut.—*Mrs. J. C. Tyler.*

OMELET—No. 2.

Six eggs, one tablespoonful of flour in one cup of milk, one teaspoonful of melted butter, one teaspoonful of salt. Yolks and whites beaten separately.—*Miss A. E. Goodrich.*

OMELET SOUFFLE.

Add to the yolks of three eggs, well beaten, four tablespoonfuls of sugar and the juice and rind of a lemon. Beat the whites of six eggs to the stiffest possible froth. Have the yolks in a deep bowl; add the whites to the mixture. Bake in a well-buttered earthen dish from fifteen to twenty minutes in a moderate oven. Serve immediately, or it will fall.—*Ellen Hand,* Providence.

BAKED OMELET.

Heat three gills of milk, with a dessert spoonful of butter. Wet a tablespoonful of flour with a tablespoonful of milk. Mix with five eggs, yolks and whites beaten separately, and stir quickly into the milk. Put into a buttered dish and bake fifteen minutes.—*Mrs. J. F. Davis.*

TOMATO OMELET.

Five eggs, four small or three large tomatoes, one-half cup of milk, one teaspoonful of flour, one scant teaspoonful of salt, half a teaspoonful of black pepper. Beat the eggs. Stir flour, salt and pepper into the milk, and add to the eggs. Peel the tomatoes, chop into small pieces, and add just before turning into the omelet pan.—*Mrs. R. H. Seeley.*

DEVILED EGGS.

Boil six or eight eggs hard, leave them in cold water until cold, remove the shells, cut them in halves, slicing a bit from the bottom to make them stand upright; take out the yolks and rub to a smooth paste, with a very little melted butter, a little cayenne pepper, a touch of mustard, salt, and a teaspoonful of vinegar. Fill the hollowed whites with this. Chop lettuce or white cabbage, seasoned with pepper, salt, vinegar, and a little sugar; fill your salad bowl with this; add the eggs and serve.

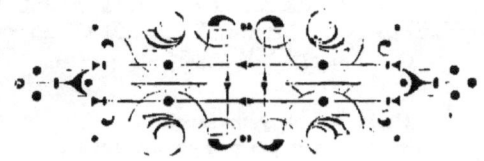

SAUCES AND SALADS.

> "Cook, see all your sauces
> Be sharp and pungent to the palate,
> That they may commend you."
>
> BEAUMONT AND FLETCHER.

SALAD DRESSING.

To make this condiment, your poet begs
The powdered yellow of two hard-boiled eggs;
Two boiled potatoes passed through kitchen sieve,
Smoothness and softness to the salad give;
Let onion's atoms lurk within the bowl,
And, half suspected, animate the whole;
Of mordant mustard, add a single spoon;
Distrust the condiment that bites so soon;
But deem it not, thou man of herbs, a fault
To add a double quantity of salt;
Four times the spoon with oil from Lucas crown,
And twice with vinegar, procured from town;
And lastly, o'er the flavored compound toss
A magic "soupcon" of anchovy sauce.
O, green and glorious, O herbaceous treat!
'Twould tempt the dying anchorite to eat;
Back to the world he'd turn his fleeting soul,
And plunge his fingers in the salad bowl;
Serenely full, the epicure would say,
"Fate cannot harm me, I have dined today."

SIDNEY SMITH.

SALAD DRESSING—No. 1.

One large tablespoonful of mixed mustard, the yolks of two eggs; rub smooth and add five tablespoonfuls of sweet oil, then the yolks of two more eggs; when smooth, five more tablespoonfuls of oil, then two more yolks and two tablespoonfuls of oil; then a little salt, half a cup of vinegar, and the whites of five eggs, well beaten.—*Mrs. Dr. Crowell.*

SALAD DRESSING—No. 2.

Three eggs, one tablespoonful each of sugar, oil, and salt, a a scant tablespoonful of mustard, a cupful of milk, a cupful of vinegar. Stir oil, salt, mustard and sugar in a bowl until perfectly smooth. Add the eggs, and beat well; then add the vinegar, and finally the milk. Place the bowl in a basin of boiling water, and stir the dressing until it thickens like soft custard. This dressing will keep two weeks, if bottled and put in cool place.—*Mrs. John P. Gilman.*

SALAD DRESSING—No. 3.

One egg well beaten, one-third of a cup of vinegar, one small teaspoonful each of sugar and mustard, a pinch of cayenne pepper, and a piece of butter as large as a walnut. Steam until it thickens, stirring constantly. When cool, add cream or milk until like soft custard.—*Mrs. S. Stuart.*

SALAD DRESSING—No. 4.

Rub the yolk of one hard-boiled egg as smooth as possible, then add a tablespoonful of butter and the yolk of one raw egg, a teaspoonful each of salt; mustard and sugar, and a tablespoonful of flour. Rub all together until perfectly smooth, then add by degrees one teacup of vinegar, (less, if strong,) and last of all, one teacup of cream whipped to a froth.—*Mrs. M. F. Ames.*

SALAD DRESSING—No. 5.

Ingredients: One tablespoonful of vinegar, three tablespoonfuls of olive oil, one salt-spoonful of salt, one of pepper, one even teaspoonful of onions scraped fine. Mix the pepper and salt, add the oil and onion, then the vinegar; when well mingled, pour the mixture over the salad and mix all together. This is especially nice for lettuce.—*Mrs. Dudley Porter.*

CHILI SAUCE.

Two quarts of tomatoes, two green peppers and two onions chopped fine, two tablespoonfuls of salt, three tablespoonfuls of sugar, four cups of vinegar. Boil the onions and peppers in the vinegar until soft, then add the tomatoes, and simmer together for nearly an hour. Add a teaspoonful of allspice, cloves and cinnamon.—*Mrs. J. S. Wheeler.*

SHIRLEY SAUCE.

Two dozen ripe tomatoes, two onions, two large red peppers, four cups of vinegar, four tablespoonfuls of sugar, three tablespoonfuls of salt. Chop peppers and onions fine. Boil all three hours slowly.—*Mrs. C. R. Evans.*

GOOD SALAD.

Chop fine half a head of cabbage. Into it stir a little salt, and half a cup of thick cream. Heat half a cup of vinegar, stirring into it the beaten yolks of two eggs, a teaspoonful of sugar, and half a teaspoonful of mustard. Pour this over the cabbage just as it goes to the table.—*Mrs. Wm. Fitz,* Providence.

TOMATO SAUCE.

One quart canned tomatoes, two tablespoonfuls of butter, two tablespoonfuls of flour, eight cloves, a small slice of onion. Cook the tomatoes, onions and cloves, ten minutes. Heat the butter in a frying-pan and add the flour. Stir over the fire until smooth and brown, and then stir into the tomatoes. Cook two minutes. Season to taste with salt and pepper, and rub through a strainer fine enough to keep back the seeds. This sauce is nice for fish, meat and macaroni.—*Mrs. John P. Gilman.*

TOMATO KETCHUP—No. 1.

One peck of ripe tomatoes, one-half pint of sugar, one-half pint of cider vinegar, one tablespoonful of salt, one teaspoonful each of allspice, ginger, black pepper and cassia, one-half teaspoonful of cayenne pepper, two teaspoonfuls of white mustard. Boil the tomatoes two hours; strain, bottle and seal.—*Mrs. E. H. Drew.*

TOMATO KETCHUP—No. 2.

One gallon of strained tomato, four even tablespoonfuls of salt, one tablespoonful and one heaping teaspoonful each of allspice, mustard, cassia and cloves, three even teaspoonfuls of red pepper, one cup of vinegar. Boil the tomatoes before straining, just enough to soften them; then add the spices, and boil away one-third—or four hours.—*Mrs. R. H. Seeley.*

CELERY SAUCE.

Cut the stalks in small pieces, boil in water, and add milk, flour, butter, a little salt and mace. Boil till it is as thick as cream.—*Mrs. Anna L. George.*

CELERY VINEGAR.

Upon an ounce of celery seed pour half a pint of vinegar. Bottle it and use to season soups and gravies.

FRENCH MUSTARD.

Slice an onion into a bowl, cover with vinegar, leave twenty-four hours, pour off the vinegar into a basin, put into it one teaspoonful of pepper and salt, one tablespoonful of brown sugar, mustard enough to thicken; smooth the mustard with vinegar, as you would for gravy. Mix it all together, set on the stove and stir until it boils. Use it cold. It will keep a long time.—*Mrs. Warner R. Whittier.*

MINT SAUCE.

Two table spoonfuls of green mint, cut fine; two of brown sugar; one-half cup of vinegar. Nice with roast lamb.—*Miss Carrie Duncan.*

BUTTER SAUCE.

Boil one teacupful of milk, and stir into it one and a half teaspoonful of flour mixed with milk or water until perfectly smooth. Let this boil two or three minutes, until it thickens a little. Add salt and a piece of butter the size of an egg, or more if you like. The butter must not be allowed to boil. Slices of hard-boiled eggs may be added, or capers to serve with boiled mutton.—*Miss S. P. Whittier.*

VEGETABLES.

"Thou unassuming commonplace of nature."—WORDSWORTH.

POTATOES.

New potatoes are best prepared just in time for cooking. Old ones should be pared, or have a strip of the skin cut off, and left in cold water for an hour or two before boiling. Put them into boiling water, salted, and keep them boiling fast. When done, drain off all the water, and let them steam very dry upon the top of the stove or in the oven. In the spring of the year they should be mashed and mixed with a little hot milk and butter. They are very nice roasted with meat. They should be pared and left in cold water for a while. About an hour before a roast of beef is done, put them in the dripping pan and baste them as the meat is basted.

SQUASH.

Squash should be steamed rather than boiled; but perhaps the best way is to cut it in large pieces and bake, then scrape from the shell and season.

BEETS.

Beets are very nice baked, but for this purpose large ones should be selected, as they shrink very much in the oven. They require from four to six hours, according to size.

PARSNIPS.

Parsnips require an hour or two to boil, and may be served simply sliced, but they are much nicer fried in butter after they have been boiled.

TURNIPS.

Turnips should be boiled in salted water, and served either sliced or mashed.

ONIONS.

Onions are best boiled in milk. If water is used, change it when they are half done. Serve whole, or in a dressing made of milk and butter, salt and pepper.

CARROTS.

Carrots, after boiling about two hours, should be cut in dice, and seasoned with butter, pepper and salt.

BEANS AND PEAS.

Beans and peas should be boiled in as little water as may be, and salted when nearly done. If the water is hard, soften it with a pinch of soda.

GREENS.

All kinds of greens should be left in cold water for an hour or two, boiled in salted water, drained in a colander, and served with slices of hard-boiled egg.

CABBAGE.

Cabbage is frequently boiled with corned beef, but a better way is to take some of the liquor from the pot and boil it by itself. Serve whole, or chop fine and cover it with butter sauce.

CAULIFLOWER.

Cauliflower should be boiled in a netting bag, in salted water, for about an hour. Serve plain or with butter sauce.

ASPARAGUS.

Asparagus will boil in half an hour. Serve very hot on slices of toast moistened with the asparagus water and generously buttered.

GREEN CORN.

Green corn should boil ten minutes, or just long enough to set the milk. Boiling after this makes it hard. If you cut it off, draw a sharp knife through each row and with the back of the knife push out the kernel, leaving the hull.

MACARONI.

Macaroni should not be washed, but the pipes may be cleaned by blowing through them. Break into short bits, put into boiling water, salted, and cook for half an hour; then drain and serve with drawn butter, or simply bits of butter and salt.

MACARONI WITH OYSTERS.

Boil macaroni in salted water and drain it through a colander. Take a deep earthen dish, and put in alternate 'layers of macaroni and oysters. Sprinkle grated cheese on the layers of macaroni. Bake until brown.

MACARONI WITH CHEESE.

Boil macaroni about twenty minutes; drain and cut in pieces. Butter a baking dish, put in a layer of macaroni, a layer of grated cheese, and a little drawn butter. Fill the dish in this way. On top put a layer of cracker crumbs with some bits of butter. Bake about twenty minutes, or until it is nicely browned. If one objects to so much cheese, the dish may be filled with macaroni, and the cheese grated over the top only.—*Miss A. S. Hobbs.*

BAKED TOMATOES.

A layer of tomatoes, peeled and sliced, layer of bread crumbs, pepper, salt, and piece of butter. Fill baking-dish in this way, with butter on top. Bake twenty minutes. Sweet corn and tomatoes prepared in the same way make a very nice dish.—*Miss A. S. Hobbs.*

SUCCOTASH.

Cut the corn from half a dozen cobs, and an hour and a half before dinner time put the cobs and a pint of shelled beans into cold water to boil. Half an hour before serving take out the cobs and put in the corn. Season with salt and pepper, and if you choose add butter and milk when you are ready to take it up.

SPINACH.

Boil in water fifteen minutes. When tender drain thoroughly, chop fine, put in a sauce-pan with two or three tablespoonfuls of milk and a small piece of butter. Stir until hot.—*Katrina Peterson.*

SARATOGA FRIED POTATOES.

Pare the potatoes and cut them into *very* thin slices. Put them in ice-water over night and fry in boiling lard, as you would doughnuts. When taken from the frying-pan put them into a napkin or towel, thus absorbing all the fat which may remain on them.

ESCALOPED POTATOES.

Cut raw potatoes in thin slices; put them in a buttered pudding-dish; sprinkle on each layer a little pepper, salt, and bits of butter.

Fill the dish three-fourths full; cover with milk and bake slowly two hours. A few bread or cracker crumbs spread over the top layer of potatoes may be added, if desired.—*Mrs. L. E. Whittier.*

STEWED CELERY.

Take a head of celery, strip off the leaves, clean and scrape the stalks thoroughly, and cut into pieces about an inch long. Boil moderately in water about three hours, or until tender; lift from the water, drain thoroughly, and pour over a dressing of water thickened with flour, to which add a piece of butter and a little salt. Serve hot.—*Mrs. J. B. Swett.*

RICE.

Wash the rice by rubbing hard between the hands in cold water. Put a cupful of rice, a teaspoonful of salt, and a pint and a half of milk and water into a milk-boiler, and boil without stirring until it is dry—probably a little more than an hour.—*Mrs. S. W. W.*

A BLACK MAN'S RECIPE TO DRESS RICE.

Wash him well, much wash in cold water, the rice flour make him stick. Water boil already very fast. Throw him in, rice can't burn, water shake him too much. Boil quarter of an hour, or little more; rub one rice in thumb and finger, if all rub away, him quite done. Put rice in colander, hot water run away; pour cup of cold water on him, put back rice in saucepan, keep him covered near the fire, then rice all ready. Eat him up.

BAKED BEANS.

Soak a pint of beans in plenty of cold water over night. In the morning skim them out into a small-sized bean-pot, putting about half a pound of salt pork near the top. Fill the pot full of cold water and let it stand on the back of the stove for about two or three hours. Pour off the most of the water and fill up again with cold water, adding a pinch of soda, and put into an oven so moderately heated that they will be at least an hour coming to the boiling point; after that the heat may be increased. They will be sufficiently cooked at supper time. Add hot water if necessary. When nearly done, taste to see if they need salt.

"To know
That which before us lies in daily life
Is the power of wisdom."
MILTON.

Good housekeepers are specially anxious to supply their families with good bread, and this cannot be done without good materials. The flour known as the new process, or Haxall flour, is unquestionably the best for bread. It costs a little more than the St. Louis, or old process flour, but as it swells more in mixing, it is quite as economical. The best results in cakes and pastry, as well as cream of tartar biscuit, are secured by the St. Louis flour; it is therefore necessary to keep both kinds in our houses.

The second requisite for good bread is good yeast. There are several varieties of yeast cake in the market which can be depended upon. The favorite in this vicinity seems to be the Vienna Compressed Yeast Cake, which is very sure if used fresh and with care as to quantity. If too much is used it will impart a disagreeable flavor to the bread. We give below three rules for liquid yeast; all excellent, easily made, and if kept in a cool place, retaining their virtues for several weeks.

If cream of tartar and soda are used, great care should be exercised in the measurement, and also in the purchase of these articles, as they are very liable to adulteration. Some of our druggists and grocers make a specialty of them, and may be relied upon to furnish them pure.

Baking powder seems to be coming into favor as a substitute for these articles, and if the variety is good may be used with excellent results. We quote from Hall's Journal of Health for April, 1882, the following government analysis of two of the leading baking powders:—

"I have examined samples of 'Cleveland's Superior Baking Powder,' and 'Royal Baking Powder,' purchased by myself in this city, and I find they contain:

CLEVELAND'S SUPERIOR BAKING POWDER—
    Cream of Tartar
    Bicarbonate of Soda
    Flour

Available carbonic acid gas, 12.61 per cent, equivalent to 118.2 cubic inches of gas per oz. of powder.

ROYAL BAKING POWDER—
    Cream of Tartar
    Bicarbonate of Soda
    Carbonate of Ammonia
    Tartaric Acid
    Starch

Available carbonic acid gas, 12.40 per cent, equivalent to 116.2 cubic inches of gas per oz. of powder.

Ammonia gas, 0.43 per cent, equivalent to 10.4 cubic inches per oz. of powder.

NOTE.—The Tartaric acid was doubtless introduced as free acid, but subsequently combined with ammonia, and exists in the powder as a Tartrate of Ammonia.

E. G. LOVE, Ph. D.

NEW YORK, Jan'y 17th, 1881.

The above shows conclusively that 'Cleveland's Superior' is a strictly pure Cream of Tartar Baking Powder. It has also been analyzed by Prof. Johnson, of Yale College; Dr. Genth, of the University of Pennsylvania; President Morton, of the Stevens Institute; Wm. M. Habirshaw, F. C. S., Analyst for the Chemical Trade of New York, and other eminent chemists, all of whom pronounce it absolutely pure and healthful."

Some persons consider much kneading essential to excellence in bread, but a little skillful kneading and cutting with a chopping knife just before it goes into the baking-pans will suffice to make it tender. The loaves should be kept in a warm place until they are about twice as large as when first taken out, and then baked in a pretty hot oven, from forty to sixty minutes, according to size. Cover with paper or a slide when the crust has attained the right color.

The best baking-pans for bread are made of Russia iron. When the loaves come from the oven they should be tilted against the pans, so as to have a free circulation of air all around them. After being thus exposed for eight or ten hours, they may be put away in closely covered tin boxes or stone jars.

YEAST—No. 1.

Grate a half-dozen large potatoes into a deep earthen dish; pour on some hot water and boil for a few minutes, stirring all the time with a silver spoon, until it is of the consistency of thick cream. Add one-third of a cupful of salt and one-third of a cupful of sugar. Cool to about blood heat, add a cupful of yeast and keep it in a warm place until risen, then cork it tight in a bottle, or keep it in a preserving jar.—*Miss Susan Johnson,* Brunswick, Me.

YEAST—No. 2.

Pare and quarter two large potatoes, and boil in nearly a quart of water; when soft mix thoroughly with two large tablespoonfuls of flour, two of sugar, and one teaspoonful of salt, then pour the water in which the potatoes were boiled over the mixture; when nearly cold add one teacupful of baker's yeast, and set in a warm place to rise. When risen, bottle and keep in a cool place.—*Mrs. A. A. Johnson.*

YEAST—No. 3.

Upon a tablespoonful of the best Shaker pressed hops put one pint of cold water and one pint of hot water; let them just come to boil, and strain upon a cupful of grated raw potato, a scant half cupful of salt, and a quarter of a cupful of sugar; let this come to boil, stirring carefully, and when nearly cold add a cupful of yeast and let it stand in a warm place till well risen; then bottle.—*Mrs. E. W. Ames.*

RAISED BREAD—No. 1.

Two quarts of flour, one tablespoonful of lard, salted, one teacupful of yeast, (No. 2,) scalded milk or milk and water enough to mix the flour; stir with a knife and cut the dough freely. Rise over night; in the morning cut the dough again and add a little soda; mould, and rise a few minutes in pans. This quantity will make two loaves and a small pan of biscuit.—*Mrs. A. A. Johnson.*

RAISED BREAD—No. 2.

A quart of warm milk and water, in the proportion of two-thirds milk to one-third water; a tablespoonful of butter, a teaspoonful of salt, a half cupful of yeast, (No. 3,) in which a pinch of soda has been dissolved. Stir in flour with a broad, strong knife, to make a moderately stiff dough; cover close and set away to rise. In the morning take out upon a moulding-board, knead a little, and cut with a chopping-knife, which makes it tender. Take out into loaves or cut into biscuit. Set them in a warm place till light. Bake in an oven hot enough to brown them in ten or fifteen minutes, then cover with a paper until done. The milk used should always have been previously scalded, and then the dough may be kept in a cool place for several days, and baked as it may be needed.

Nice Graham Bread may be made by taking a piece of this dough, when very light, large enough for half a loaf. Work into it, with the hand, a little soda dissolved in half a cup of milk, add salt and molasses, and enough Graham meal to stiffen it. Knead a very little and rise again.—*Mrs. C. W. Train.*

RYE BREAD—No. 1.

One quart of bolted rye, one pint of flour, two tablespoonfuls of Indian meal, one-half cup of yeast; moisten with milk to the stiffness of flour bread, set it to rise and treat it like raised flour bread.—*Mrs. John Keely*, Kingston.

RYE BREAD—No. 2.

One quart of rye flour, one pint of wheat flour, one pint of milk and water, two-thirds of a cup of yeast, a little salt; stir this up at night; in the morning add one egg, one-half cup of sugar, one tablespoonful of butter, a small teaspoonful of soda; stir all thoroughly together, and put in a pan to rise. Let it rise one hour, and then bake.—*Mrs. J. V. Smiley.*

BREAD FROM GLUTEN FLOUR.

Into about two quarts of gluten flour put a little salt, a cup two-thirds full of yeast. Before going to bed set the sponge with about one and one-half pints of milk or water; in the morning knead the sponge and put in about one tablespoonful of sugar and one of lard, and a quarter of a teaspoonful of soda; keep in a warm place, and when it becomes light, knead again and put into pans to rise. Use your judgment about kneading. When it becomes light in the pans, put it in a moderately heated oven and bake from three-fourths of an hour to an hour. This will make two large loaves. *It works equally well without the sugar, lard and soda, and for diabetics sugar must be omitted.*

BROWN BREAD—No. 1.

One egg, one cup of sour milk and two cups of sweet milk, or three cups of sweet milk, two-thirds cup of molasses, one heaping cup of Graham meal, one cup of rye, one cup of Indian meal, one teaspoonful of soda, a little salt. Steam three hours, then set in the oven twenty minutes.—*Mrs. J. Houston West.*

BROWN BREAD—No. 2.

One and one-half cup of Indian meal, the same of rye, one cup of flour, two-thirds of a cup of molasses, nearly three cups of milk, or milk and water, one teaspoonful of soda, and a little salt. Steam four hours, then take off the cover and let it stand in the oven fifteen minutes.—*Mrs. Helen A. Chase.*

BROWN BREAD—No. 3.

One cup of molasses, one cup of Indian meal, one cup of rye, one cup of flour, three scant teaspoonfuls of soda, one of salt. Make a not *too* stiff batter with water. Butter your bread-pan, pour in the batter and steam three hours or more. Then cook in the oven half an hour.—*Maggie Donnell.*

BROWN BREAD—No. 4.

Four cups of Indian meal, one of rye meal, one of molasses, one egg, one teaspoonful of soda, one pint of water, one of milk, a little salt. Bake four hours, covered.—*Mrs. Geo. H. Appleton.*

BROWN BREAD—No. 5.

Two cups of Indian meal, one-half cup of rye meal, one cup of flour, two cups of sweet milk, one-half cup of molasses, one teaspoonful of soda, a little salt. Steam four hours.—*Mrs. Dr. Towle.*

THIRD BISCUIT.

One pint of sour milk, one teaspoonful of soda, salt, one-half cup of molasses, one-third of a cup of rye meal, Indian meal and flour, stiff enough to drop from a spoon. Bake in a hot oven.—*Mrs. Phebe How.*

RYE BISCUIT.

Two cups of rye, one cup of flour, two eggs, one teaspoonful of cream of tartar, one-half teaspoonful of soda, one tablespoonful of molasses, a little salt, milk sufficient to make a stiff batter.—*Mrs. Dr. Crowell.*

PARKER HOUSE ROLLS.

Put two quarts of flour into a pan. Make a hole in the flour and put in half a cup of yeast, a tablespoonful of sugar, a tablespoonful of butter, a little salt, and one pint of milk. When risen, mix and leave to rise again. After it has risen the second time, cut into thin, round biscuit. With a bit of cloth spread over each a little melted butter, then fold over and put in a pan. Spread a little melted butter on the top of each roll. When well risen, bake in a quick oven. Do not knead at all. — *Mrs. Jonathan Kimball.*

BREAKFAST AND TEA CAKES.

"And then to breakfast, with
What appetite you have."
SHAKSPERE.

SQUASH BREAKFAST CAKES.

One pint of sifted squash, one large tablespoonful of lard melted into the squash, two tablespoonfuls of white sugar, one-third of a compressed yeast cake dissolved in half a cup of warm water, a little salt. Stir in flour until it is as stiff as bread-dough; mould a little; let it rise over night; roll out without moulding in the morning. Make into biscuit and let them rise half an hour or more and bake fifteen minutes.—*Miss Sue E. Emerson.*

SQUASH INDIAN CAKE.

Two cups of Indian meal, one cup of sifted squash, one cup of flour, one-half cup of molasses, one teaspoonful of cream of tartar, half as much soda, a little salt. Mix in one pint of milk, and bake in a hot oven one-half hour.—*Miss Annie J. Gile.*

SQUASH ROLLS.

One pint of flour, three-fourths of a cup of sugar, one cup of sifted squash, butter the size of an English walnut, salt, one and one-third cup of milk, a teaspoonful of cream of tartar, half as much soda. Bake in a roll-pan, twenty minutes. — *Mrs. E. W. Ames.*

RYE PUFFS.

Two cups of rye meal, one of flour, one of milk, one egg, one teaspoonful of soda, two of cream of tartar, tablespoonful of sugar, a little salt. Bake in gem pan, or as griddle cakes.—*Mrs. F. A. Brown.*

POP-OVERS.

One egg, one cup of milk, one cup of flour, a little salt. Bake in gem pan or in buttered cups, filling them half full.—*Mrs. J. S. Wheeler.*

TEA CAKE.

One cup of sugar, one-half cup of butter, two eggs, one-half cup of milk, two cups of flour, one teaspoonful of cream of tartar, one-half teaspoonful of soda.—*Mrs. J. V. Smiley.*

BREAKFAST CAKE.

One quart of flour, one pint of milk, two eggs, one small cup of white sugar, two teaspoonfuls of cream of tartar, one of soda, one of salt, a piece of butter as large as an egg. Bake in gem pan or cups.—*Mrs. S. Stuart.*

GRAHAM GEMS.

One cupful of Graham flour, one of wheat flour, one egg, salt, one teaspoonful of cream of tartar, half as much soda, milk enough to make a stiff batter. Rye meal or Indian meal may be used instead of Graham flour.—*Mrs. T. G. Appleton.*

BERRY CAKE—No 1.

Two heaping bowls of flour, one of berries, one of sugar, one pint of milk, one and one-fourth teaspoonful of soda, a piece of butter size of an egg rubbed into the flour, a little salt. Bake three-quarters of an hour.—*Mrs. Wm. Jeffers.*

BERRY CAKE—No. 2.

One egg, two-thirds of a cup of sugar, one large spoonful of butter, one cup of milk, one pint of flour, two cups of berries, one-half teaspoonful of soda, one teaspoonful of cream of tartar.—*Mrs. M. F. Johnson.*

STRAWBERRY SHORT-CAKE.

A rule of cream of tartar biscuit, made quite rich with butter and sugar. Bake, split into thin slices and butter the slices. Sugar a plenty of strawberries and put between the slices. Serve hot.—*Mrs. Wm. S. Perley.*

PEACH SHORT-CAKE.

One and one-half pint of flour, two tablespoonfuls of melted butter, one pint of milk, one egg, two teaspoonfuls of cream of tartar, one of soda. Bake in two cakes, split and butter well. Spread between the layers, peaches, mashed and sugared. Pour over cream, if you like.—*Mrs. Wm. Fitz.* Providence, R. I.

CORN CAKE—No. 1.

One-half cup of sugar, two large tablespoonfuls of butter, one or two eggs, two cups of milk, two of flour, one of Indian meal, two teaspoonfuls of cream of tartar, one of soda.—*Miss Ella Moore.*

CORN CAKE—No. 2.

Two eggs, one-half cup of sugar, two cups of sour milk, two of Indian meal, one of flour, a half teaspoonful of soda, salt.—*Mrs. L. Whittier.*

CORN CAKE—No. 3.

One cup of Indian meal, two of flour, two of sweet milk, one egg, one tablespoonful of white sugar, two heaping teaspoonfuls of cream of tartar, one of soda. Bake in gem pan or rings.—*Miss H. D. Newcomb.*

CORN CAKE—No. 4.

One cup of sweet milk, one heaping cup of corn meal, one tablespoonful of flour, a pinch of salt, a teaspoonful of Cleveland's superior baking powder. The meal should be fine, and the cake must not be overdone in the least.—*Mrs. Wm. Brooks.*

INDIAN CUP CAKES.

One coffee cup of Indian meal, a piece of butter size of half an egg, salt, scalded with one pint of boiling milk; add three eggs, whites and yolks beaten separately. Bake immediately in cups.—*Mrs. C. W. Train.*

INDIAN DROP CAKES.

One pint of *white* Indian meal, teaspoonful of salt, butter big as half an egg. Scald thoroughly. Add two eggs, well beaten, and milk until it will just drop from a spoon. Bake in a hot oven, dropped upon a pan, or in gem pans.—*Mrs. C. W. Train.*

WHITE INDIAN BANNOCK.

One pint of *white* Indian, one pint of milk, one pint of water, one tablespoonful of sugar, one teaspoonful of salt. Boil the milk and water together and pour it over the meal. When thoroughly mixed, return to the kettle and boil till it is thick. Then cool it, add three beaten eggs, salt and sugar, and bake.—*Miss E. H. Train,* Newton Centre.

DUTCH APPLE CAKE.

Make a rich biscuit dough, roll about half an inch thick and put in a pan; stick thickly, sliced apples in rows over the top and sprinkle with sugar. Bake, and serve with sugar and cream.—*Mrs. Elbridge Wood.*

PAN CAKES—No. 1.

One cup of rye, one-half cup of Indian, two cups of flour, one-half cup of sugar, one-third cup of yeast, salt; mix and rise. When risen, add an egg, and fry in boiling lard.—*Miss Sallie Swan.*

PAN CAKES—No. 2.

Two cups of milk, two cups of rye, two-thirds cup of Indian meal, one-third cup of flour, one egg, one teaspoonful of soda, two tablespoonfuls of sugar, (or one-third cup of molasses,) and a little salt.—*Mrs. J. K. Smith.*

PAN CAKES—No. 3.

One egg, one cup of sugar, one cup of milk, two teaspoonfuls of cream of tartar, one of soda, a little salt and nutmeg; mix quite stiff with flour.—*Mrs. Wm. Jeffers.*

PAN CAKES—No. 4.

One pint of milk, two eggs, one cup of sugar, one teaspoonful of soda, a little salt, one-third Indian meal, two-thirds rye flour.—*Mrs. Phebe How.*

SWEET APPLE PANCAKES.

Pare and chop four sweet apples. Stir them into batter made of one egg, two tablespoonfuls of molasses and one of brown sugar, a little salt, one cup of sour milk, two-thirds of a teaspoonful of soda, one-half cup of rye meal, one and one-half cup of rye flour. Fry in hot lard.—*Mrs. Susan Kimball.*

JOLLY BOYS.

Two cups of Indian meal, one-half cup of sugar, and a little salt. Pour boiling water over it, and stir until a thick dough. When cool, add one well-beaten egg, one cup of flour, one-half teaspoonful of soda. Fry like pancakes, in boiling lard.—*Mrs. Chas. B. Emerson.*

APPLE FRITTERS.

Make a batter of one egg, one cup of milk, flour to make as stiff as common fritters, a little salt. Stir into the batter about one pint of chopped apples. Fry as you do pancakes. Sugar them as you take them out.—*Mrs. L. W. Johnson.*

DOUGHNUTS—No. 1.

One egg, three-fourths of a cup of sugar, piece of butter half the size of an egg, one cup of sweet milk, very small teaspoonful of soda, one cup of yeast, flour to make it as stiff as you can stir with a spoon, a little nutmeg and cinnamon; rise over night.—*Mrs. Josiah Brown.*

DOUGHNUTS—No. 2.

Butter size of an egg, one egg, coffee cup of milk, large coffee cup of sugar, salt, spice, if you please; half cupful of yeast, pinch of soda, flour enough to make it as stiff as bread.—*Mrs. Rebecca Hale.*

DOUGHNUTS—No. 3.

Two eggs, one cup of sugar, butter size of half an egg, cup of milk, one-half teaspoonful of soda, one teaspoonful of cream of tartar, spice to taste, flour to roll.—*Miss S. E. Fitts.*

DOUGHNUTS—No. 4.

Teacup of sour cream, one teaspoonful of soda, one cup of sugar, three eggs, flour enough to roll, a little salt and spice.—*Mrs. Spring,* Portland.

MIRACLES.

Three eggs, three tablespoonfuls of melted butter; mix with flour to roll thin, sprinkle over sugar, cut in squares, double together and cut long slits, then take every other link on the forefinger and slip from the finger into boiling lard.—*Mrs. J. F. Davis.*

GRIDDLE CAKES.

Sour milk, soda enough to sweeten it, a little salt, a very little melted butter, flour to make a thin batter. Have ready a hot griddle, and try a spoonful to see that it is right before cooking the whole. They are very nice thickened in part with Graham meal, boiled rice, hominy, or bread crumbs. Add eggs, if you choose, but they are more delicate and tender without them. Very nice griddle cakes are made by mixing Graham meal with milk and yeast at night, and frying in the morning, just like buckwheats.

OATMEAL GRIDDLE CAKES.

One pint of oatmeal mush, one pint of flour, two eggs, piece of butter the size of an egg, one and one-half pint of sour milk or buttermilk, a teaspoonful of soda dissolved in boiling water just before baking.—*Miss Maria Beach*, Framingham.

INDIAN GRIDDLE CAKES.

Two cups white corn meal, one cup of flour, one-half cup of yeast, one teaspoonful of salt; milk added to make a stiff batter; put in a warm place to rise over night, as a sponge for bread.—*Mrs. T. T. Munger*, No. Adams.

RYE GRIDDLE CAKES.

One cup of sweet milk, one egg, salt, enough rye flour to make a batter, one teaspoonful of cream of tartar sifted into the flour, half a teaspoonful of soda dissolved in the milk.—*Julia A. Marshall, M. D.*

MUFFINS—No. 1.

Two cups of rye meal, one cup of flour, two cups of sour milk, soda sufficient to sweeten, two eggs, three teaspoonfuls of molasses, a little salt.

Indian muffins may be made by the same rule, substituting Indian for rye and sugar for molasses.—*Mrs. John Keeley*, Kingston.

MUFFINS—No. 2.

One pint of milk, two eggs, piece of butter half as large as an egg, a little salt, flour enough to make a batter as for griddle cakes, yeast enough to make it rise in a few hours. Pour into rings, and bake on the griddle.—*Mrs. Phineas Webster*, Bradford.

MUFFINS—No. 3.

One egg, one tablespoonful of sugar, one of butter, a pinch of salt; stir to a cream. Add three cups of sweet milk. To two cups of fine flour add two cups of gluten and four teaspoonfuls of Cleveland's superior baking powder. Stir slowly into the milk and bake in hot gem pans in a hot oven.—*Mrs. A. H. Strong*, Rochester, N. Y.

MUFFINS—No. 4.

One cup of sour milk, half a teaspoonful of soda, one tablespoonful of molasses, one of melted butter, one cup of Graham flour, one-half cup of wheat flour, a little salt. Bake in a quick oven.—*Mrs. A. H. Herring.*

MUFFINS—No. 5.

One pint of milk, one tablespoonful of rice flour, butter (melted) size of half an egg, salt, dessertspoonful of sugar, yeast and flour to make a batter. Just before frying, add one egg, well beaten, and a pinch of soda.—*Mrs. Chadwick.*

WAFFLES.

One and one-half pint of milk, four and one-half cups of flour, two-thirds cup of butter, two eggs, one-half cup of Indian meal, a little salt, and one-half cup of yeast.—*Miss R. Blaisdell*, Boston.

BRUISS.

Take crusts of brown bread, and if they are hard and dry, lay them over night in a little water. In the morning add milk and boil slowly. Sprinkle in salt, and just before serving add a little butter. It is improved by adding a little white bread.

COTTAGE CHEESE.

Set away a quart or more of skimmed milk to sour. When it has just thickened, pour into it about as much boiling water, and leave it for half an hour; then strain through a cloth. Salt the curd and it is ready to serve.

CORN OYSTERS.

One pint of sweet corn, grated; one egg, well beaten; small cup of flour, teaspoonful of salt; mix well together and fry like oysters.

FRIED BANANAS.

Add a little milk to a well-beaten egg, and have ready some finely pounded and sifted bread crumbs and a kettle of boiling lard. Skin the bananas and dip them (whole) into the egg and then into crumbs, and fry from three to five minutes, until they are of a delicate brown color.—*Miss A. B. Train*, Newton Centre.

OATMEAL.

Stir a cupful of steam-cooked oatmeal and a little salt into about a pint of boiling water. Let it cook without more stirring, until the water is absorbed—about half an hour. Putting it into cold water, and too much stirring, injure both flavor and consistency. The easiest way is to cook it in a milk-boiler.

CRISPED CRACKER.

Split common crackers; butter them well. Lay them buttered side up in baking-pans and brown in a quick oven. Good either hot or cold.

FRENCH TOAST.

One pint of milk, two eggs, a little salt. Put slices of very light bread into the custard for a few minutes, then put them upon a hot buttered griddle, turning them to brown both sides. Eat with butter and sugar.—*Mrs. C. W. Train.*

APPLE SLUMP—No. 1.

Fill a large-sized bean-pot with tart apples cut in quarters. Add sufficient molasses to nearly cover them, and a teaspoonful of allspice; cover the top with brown bread; bake three hours, then cut the bread into the apples and bake one-half hour longer. Serve when hot, with cream.—*Mrs. F. A. Brown.*

APPLE SLUMP—No. 2.

Fill a three-pint dish nearly full of pared and quartered apples of some variety that will cook easily. Add a cupful each of molasses and sugar, half a cupful of water, some bits of butter and a little cinnamon. Cover with a cream of tartar crust, a little richer and softer than for biscuit. Steam an hour and a half. Pour upside down into a deep pudding-dish and serve immediately.

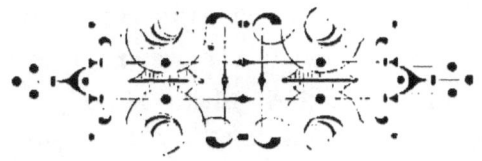

PIES.

On Thanksgiving day, when from East and from West,
From North and from South come the pilgrim and guest,
When the gray-haired New Englander sees round his board
The old broken links of affection restored,
When the care-wearied man seeks his mother once more,
And the worn matron smiles where the girl smiled before,
What moistens the lip and what brightens the eye,
What calls back the past, like the rich pumpkin pie?

WHITTIER.

PUFF PASTE—No. 1.

One quart of flour, one cup of lard cut in with a knife, one teaspoonful of salt; add enough ice water to make a stiff paste; then take one cup of butter, divide into four parts, roll in, sprinkling each time with flour.—*Mrs. J. V. Smiley.*

PUFF PASTE—No. 2.

One pound of flour and a pound of butter. Work the butter with a spoon until it is soft and pliable. Divide it into four equal parts, and with a knife cut one part into the flour. Mix with a very little ice water; take it out upon the moulding-board;

pound it with the rolling-pin until it adheres sufficiently to roll out; add the second portion of butter, then the third and fourth. Put it upon the ice to cool; and it is better to stand over night before using.—*Mrs. F. M. Sabine*, Bangor, Me.

PUFF PASTE—No. 3.

Two pounds of flour, one and one-fourth pounds of butter. Rub one-third of the butter into one-half of the flour, reserving the remainder of the flour to roll in with the balance of the butter. Use no more than the weight of flour.—*Mrs. S. L. Holt.*

SHELLS FOR TARTS—No. 1.

One and a quarter pound of butter, two pounds of flour. Stir one egg into one and one-half pound of the flour. Stir up stiff with water, roll out, put the butter in the centre and roll out three times.—*Mrs. M. Steele.*

SHELLS FOR TARTS—No. 2.

Into a pint of flour sift one teaspoonful of cream of tartar and one-half teaspoonful of soda. Rub lightly into it one cup of butter; mix with half a cup of milk. Bake in a quick oven. This quantity makes twenty-five tarts.—*Mrs. Jas. Noyes.*

MINCE PIES—No. 1.

Three pounds of meat, six of apples, one and one-half of suet, three of raisins, and four of sugar; four nutmegs, three lemons, ground cloves and cinnamon. Moisten as you please.—*Mrs. Abel Page.*

MINCE PIES—No. 2.

Four pounds each of meat, apples, suet, raisins, and sugar, five nutmegs and other spice to taste.—*Mrs. J. K. Smith.*

MINCE PIES—No. 3.

Two one-half pounds meat after it is boiled, one pound of pork, one-half pound of butter, two pounds of raisins, two and three-quarters pounds of apples, two and one-half pounds sugar. Mixing and spice to the taste.—*Mrs. S. L. Holt.*

MOCK MINCE MEAT.

Three pounded crackers, one cup of sugar, two cups of water, one-half cup each of vinegar and melted butter, cup of raisins, salt and spice to taste.

SQUASH PIE.

Steam the squash, and rub through a hair sieve. Allow two or three eggs to each pie, and beat them very light indeed; then beat eggs and squash together. Add milk, sugar, and salt. Flavor with vanilla, ginger, or mace.

GRANDMOTHER'S PUMPKIN PIE.

Five pounds of pumpkin, stewed and strained, two quarts scalded milk, two-thirds of a cup of molasses, one-half cup of brown sugar, two teaspoonfuls of ginger, a little salt.

Pastry made of cream, or one pint of flour, one tablespoonful of lard and one of butter, one teaspoonful of cream of tartar, and half as much soda. Bake two hours.—*Mrs. F. A. Brown.*

SWEET POTATO PIE.

Boil two good-sized sweet potatoes, and when tender rub through the colander. Beat the yolks of three eggs light; stir with a pint of milk into the potatoes; add a small teacup of sugar, a pinch of salt, and flavor with lemon. Bake like pumpkin pie. When done make a meringue top with the whites of the eggs and powdered sugar; brown a moment in the oven.—*Miss A. G. Beckwith.*

APPLE PIE.

Stew the apples in as little water as possible, till they are just soft; strain, sweeten and flavor to taste. One quince stewed with several apples makes a delicious sauce for pies.

The nicest apple pies are baked in deep plates, filled with slices of raw apple, sugar, and bits of butter. Cover with pastry, and have an under crust or not, as you please.

For another variety, fill a deep plate with sliced apples; add a couple spoonfuls of water; cover and bake. When done, turn out upon another plate, bringing crust down and sauce up. Serve warm, with sugar and cream.

MOCK APPLE PIE.

One large cracker broken into a small cup of water. Add juice of a lemon, and almost a cup of sugar.—*Mrs. H. Sawyer.*

MARLBORO' PIE—No. 1.

One quart of apples, ten eggs, one pound of sugar, half a pound of butter, a little grated lemon peel, and a little mace. Bake in saucers lined with rich paste.—*Mrs. A. B. Whittier.*

MARLBORO' PIE No. 2.

One cup of stewed and sifted apple, one cup of sugar, one of milk, two tablespoonfuls of melted butter, yolks of three eggs. Make the frosting of the whites of the eggs, and brown in the oven.—*T.*

DATE PIE—No. 1.

The yolks of three eggs and one cup of sugar beaten well together, one cup of stoned and chopped dates, one cup of cream, a small piece of butter; flavor with nutmeg. After chopping the dates, lay them around on the bottom crust, then beat the sugar and eggs well together, add the cream and pour all on to the plate; cut in a small piece of butter, grate a very little nutmeg, cover and bake. Beat the whites of the eggs to a stiff froth, and use for frosting the pie.—*Miss Lizzie Swasey.*

DATE PIE—No. 2.

Stone one pound of molasses dates, simmer fifteen minutes in water enough to cover them, strain, add one quart of milk and four well-beaten eggs. Bake with only an under crust. This will make two good-sized pies.—*Miss Annie J. Gile.*

LEMON PIE—No. 1.

One teacup of powdered sugar, one tablespoonful of butter, one egg, the juice and grated rind of one lemon, one teacup of boiling water, and one tablespoonful of corn starch dissolved in cold water. Stir the corn starch into the boiling water, cream the butter and sugar and pour over them the hot mixture. When quite cool, add lemon and the beaten egg, grating the rind of the lemon and chopping the pulp. Bake without top crust.—*Mrs. S. Stuart.*

LEMON PIE—No. 2.

One lemon, one egg, one cup of sugar, one tablespoonful of corn starch wet in cold water, and a teacupful of boiling water poured over it to thicken. Cover a plate with paste, put in a layer of fresh apples sliced very thin, then pour the lemon over. Cover with paste and bake.—*Mrs. Moses W. Putnam.*

LEMON PIE—No. 3.

Juice of two lemons, grated rind of one, ten tablespoonfuls of sugar, yolks of three eggs, and two tablespoonfuls of corn starch. Frost with the whites of the eggs.—*Mrs. D. F. Fitts.*

LEMON PIE—No. 4.

One cup of sugar, the yolks of two large or three small eggs; save the whites for frosting. After the eggs and sugar are well beaten, squeeze the juice of one lemon into it. Take a large half pint of milk, set on the stove, and when it is scalded, stir in one small tablespoonful of corn starch, wet in cold milk; add the egg and sugar. Bake in a deep plate, with a nice paste, putting an edge around the plate. After it is baked, beat the whites of the eggs to a stiff froth, put in about two teaspoonfuls of sugar, and spread lightly over the pie, and brown in the oven.—*Mrs. Leverett Johnson.*

LEMON TARTS.

The juice and grated rind of a lemon, the yolk of an egg, a cup of sugar; mix all together. Upon this pour a cup of cold water, into which has been stirred a dessertspoonful of corn starch. Stir all in a hot sauce-pan until it becomes a clear jelly. With this fill the shells which have been already baked. Frost with the white of the egg, and slightly brown.—*T.*

RAISIN TARTS.

One heaping coffee-cup of stoned and chopped raisins, two small cups of powdered sugar, two lemons, grated rind and juice. Put all together in a bowl and set in the teakettle till the sugar is dissolved. When cool, fill the shells.—*Mrs. George W. Duncan.*

CHESS PIES.

Take the inside of one lemon and chop fine; one cup of chopped raisins, one of sugar, one egg; mix together. Make a nice paste, roll thin and cut in squares, wet the edges with milk and fill with the above ingredients; lap the edges and press ends with fork; cut smoothly. Bake in a quick oven.—*Mrs. I. Brown.*

BRAMBERRIES.

One lemon and one cup of raisins, chopped fine; one cup of sugar, one egg, small piece of butter, filling for pastry.—*Mrs. J. K. Collins.*

PUDDINGS.

"The proof of the pudding is in the eating."

EVE'S PUDDING.

"If you want a good pudding, mind what you are taught;
Take eggs six in number when bought for a groat;
The fruit with which Eve her husband did cozen,
Well pared and well chopped, at least half a dozen;
Six ounces of bread, let Madge eat the crust,
And crumble the rest as fine as the dust;
Six ounces of currants from the stems you must sort,
Lest you break out your teeth and spoil all the sport;
Six ounces of sugar won't make it too sweet;
Some salt and some nutmeg will make it complete;
Three hours let it boil without any flutter;
But Adam won't like it without sauce or butter."

THANKSGIVING PLUM PUDDING.

Ten ounces of baker's bread, six ounces of sugar, a quarter of a pound of butter, one pint of milk, eight eggs, one pound stoned raisins, a quarter of a pound of currants, three-eighths of a pound of citron, a nutmeg and a half, half teaspoonful of soda, salt. Remove the crust and grate the bread. Put a layer of bread in a buttered dish, then butter cut in small pieces, then a layer of the fruit; so proceed till within two inches of the top of the dish. Beat the sugar and eggs thoroughly, add the milk, nutmegs, salt and soda. Pour this custard slowly into the dish, absorbing the bread gradually. Let it stand two or three hours and then bake about two hours.—*Mrs. S. Phillips.*

BOILED ENGLISH PLUM PUDDING.

One pound of flour, half pound of raisins, two and one-half pounds of currants, two ounces of citron, one teacupful of brown sugar, one of molasses, five eggs, one-quarter of a pound of chopped suet moistened with milk. Add nutmeg, clove and salt. Mix with milk a little thicker than batter. Steam or boil five or six hours.—*Mrs. Jas. R. Nichols.*

BAKED PLUM PUDDING.

Upon five crackers, well buttered, and a cupful of sugar, pour a quart of boiling milk and let it stand over night. In the morning break up the crackers, add three well-beaten eggs, salt, spice and raisins. Bake two or three hours. If you please, increase the eggs and butter.—*Mrs. C. W. Train.*

PLAIN PLUM PUDDING.

One loaf of Graham bread soaked in one quart of scalded milk, four ounces of suet, chopped fine; one pound of fruit, raisins, currants, citron; one tablespoonful of salt, three eggs, nutmeg. Boil five hours and serve with foaming sauce.—*Mrs. J. B. C.*

SUET PUDDING.

Three cups of flour, one of milk, one of molasses, one large cup of suet chopped fine, one cup of raisins, currants and citron, teaspoonful of every kind of spice, a little salt, one teaspoonful of soda stirred into the molasses. Boil three hours constantly in pudding boiler.—*Miss J. F. Smiley.*

YORK PUDDING.

Three cups of flour, one of suet or butter, one of currants or raisins, one of molasses, one of sweet milk, one egg, one teaspoonful of soda, spice to taste. Steam four hours. Cold sauce preferable.—*Mrs. W. F. Evans.*

BERRY PUDDING—No. 1.

One cup of sour milk, one of molasses, one egg, flour to make a stiff batter, one teaspoonful of soda, scant quart of berries. Steam three hours.—*Miss Carrie Duncan.*

BERRY PUDDING—No. 2.

One quart of flour, large tablespoonful of butter rubbed in, salt, two well-beaten eggs, two teaspoonfuls of cream of tartar, half as much soda. Mix quite soft with milk. A pint and a half of berries. Steam four hours.—*Mrs. C. S. W.*

BERRY PUDDING—No. 3.

One pint of flour, one pint of berries, one cup of molasses and milk, half and half; sour milk, if you have it; salt, and a small teaspoonful of soda. Steam three hours. Serve with sauce.—*Mrs. W. R. Whittier.*

STEAMED PUDDING.

One pint of flour, one-half cup of sugar, three tablespoonfuls of melted butter, one-half pint of sweet milk, one egg, one teaspoonful of soda, two of cream of tartar. Stir well together. Steam for one hour. Serve with sauce.—*Mrs. H. C. Graves.*

DANISH FLOUR PUDDING.

Two ounces of butter melted in a sauce-pan; stir in smoothly three ounces of flour; pour in slowly half a pint of boiled milk, stirring all the time over the stove, until spoon and sauce-pan are clear—it will take about half an hour. Let it cool, then drop in, one at a time, the yolks of three eggs; add the whites, beaten very light. Mace for flavoring. A teaspoonful of Cleveland's superior baking powder, the last thing. Boil two hours.—*Katrina Peterson.*

QUEEN OF PUDDINGS.

One pint of bread crumbs, one quart of milk, one cup of sugar, the yolks of four eggs, the grated rind of one lemon, a piece of butter the size of an egg. Bake like a custard. When baked, spread over the top slices of jelly, and cover the whole with the whites of the eggs beaten to a stiff froth, mixed with a cup of sugar and the juice of lemon. Brown lightly in the oven.

BREAD PUDDING.

Take fine bread crumbs and cover with warm milk in which a small piece of butter has been melted. Use one pint of crumbs to one pint of milk, three eggs, one cup of sugar, and whatever flavor you like. Bake quickly in a buttered dish. A cup of desiccated cocoanut is very nice in this pudding.—*Mrs. E. W. Ames.*

INDIAN PUDDING—No. 1.

One quart of boiling milk, one cup of Indian meal, one of molasses, two tablespoonfuls of melted butter, one teaspoonful of salt. Scald meal and milk well together, add the other ingredients and let it stand till quite cold. Pour into a buttered dish and add a pint of cold milk without stirring. Bake three hours. Serve with cream or milk.—*Mrs. S. S. Hunking.*

INDIAN PUDDING—No. 2.

One cup of Indian meal, one cup of molasses; mix, and stir into a quart of boiling milk, until it thickens; add a little salt, and butter the size of an egg. Pour into a buttered pudding-dish, and when it begins to boil in the oven, add a pint of cold milk. Bake two or three hours in a moderate oven.—*Mrs. M. K. Tyler.*

INDIAN PUDDING—No. 3.

Seven tablespoonfuls of Indian meal, wet with molasses; pour over this three pints of boiling milk; when cool, add a piece of butter the size of an egg, then three well beaten eggs, and a little salt; spice with cinnamon and ginger. Bake two and one-half hours.—*Mrs. J. F. Davis.*

INDIAN PUDDING No. 4.

One quart of scalded milk, one-half cup of Indian meal, one-fourth cup of flour. Wet flour and meal with a very little cold milk, and stir it into the scalded milk. When cool, add two eggs, one-half cup of sugar, one-fourth cup of molasses, nutmeg and salt. Rub a piece of butter as large as half an egg, around the pan before putting in the pudding. Sliced apples spread over the top give a nice flavor. Bake two hours in moderate oven.—*Mrs. M. L. Stover.*

INDIAN PUDDING—No. 5.

Pour a quart of boiling milk upon seven heaping spoonfuls of Indian meal, half a teaspoonful of salt, and two spoonfuls of ginger or cinnamon. Mix well, and just before setting it in the oven, stir in a cup of cold water, which will produce the same effect as eggs. Bake three-quarters of an hour in a deep dish.—*Mrs. J. B. C.*

TOGUS.

Three cups of sweet milk, one of sour, three cups of Indian meal, one of flour, one-half cup of molasses, small teaspoonful of soda. Steam three or four hours. Eat with butter instead of brown bread, or with sugar and cream, for a pudding.—*Mrs. C. R. T.*

BATTER PUDDING.

One cup of flour, one teaspoonful of salt, one quart of milk; stir milk into flour gradually; when mixed, add five well-beaten eggs; put into a two-quart pudding-mold and steam slowly two hours.

Sauce.—Two cups of sugar, one of butter; mix with the hand until creamy; add the flavoring, and, when ready to serve, three tablespoonfuls of boiling water.—*Lincoln House*, Swampscott.

NOTTINGHAM PUDDING.

One quart of milk, five eggs, one pint of flour, a little salt. Have the dish filled with apples, pared and cored. Pour the batter over them. Bake immediately about an hour and a half in a hot oven. Serve with sauce.—*Mrs. C. W. Train.*

SIMPLE PUDDING.

Three crackers rolled fine, one pint of milk, one-half cup of sugar, yolks of two eggs, salt and nutmeg. Bake half an hour. Beat whites to a froth with a little sugar; brown in the oven. Lay bits of jelly on the top. Serve warm.—*Mrs. Dr. S. K. Towle.*

DELMONICO PUDDING.

Three tablespoonfuls of corn starch, one quart of milk, five eggs, or less. Mix the corn starch with a little cold milk, beat the yolks of the eggs with five tablespoonfuls of sugar, add to the corn starch, and stir all into the quart of milk just before it boils; let all boil together until thickened, stirring carefully. Flavor and pour into a dish. Beat the whites of the eggs with three tablespoonfuls of sugar; spread a thin layer over the pudding and drop the remainder in little spots upon the surface; brown delicately in the oven. To be served cold.—*Mrs. E. W. Ames.*

COLD SAGO PUDDING.

Into a pint of boiling milk stir half a cup of sago, soaked in a pint of cold milk, one-half cup of sugar, and a little salt. Boil a few minutes, until the sago is transparent. Take it from the fire and add yolks of three eggs. When cold, flavor as you please, pour into a glass dish and cover with a frosting made of the whites of the eggs and two tablespoonfuls of sugar.

GREEN CORN PUDDING.

Draw a sharp knife lengthwise through each row of corn, and push out the pulp with the back of the knife blade. To one pint of the corn add one quart of milk, three eggs, a little suet or butter, sugar to taste. Stir it occasionally while baking, till it begins to thicken, and bake about two hours.—*Mrs. M. W. G.*

CHOCOLATE PUDDING.

One quart of scalded milk, one and one-half squares of grated chocolate. Wet with cold milk, and stir into the scalded milk. When the chocolate is dissolved, pour into a pudding-dish; add the yolks of six eggs, one whole egg, well-beaten, and six tablespoonfuls of sugar. Bake in a slow oven about three-quarters of an hour. It must not whey. Beat whites to a stiff froth, add sugar to taste, spread it over, and slightly brown.—*Mrs. A. H. Strong*, Rochester, N. Y.

ORANGE PUDDING—No. 1.

Six oranges cut fine; strew over them a cup of sugar and a cup of desiccated cocoanut. Beat the yolks of six eggs with four spoonfuls of corn starch, and stir into a quart of boiling milk. When it thickens, pour this over the oranges. Beat the whites of the eggs with two spoonfuls of sugar, and drop in spots upon the surface. Brown in the oven. To be eaten cold.—*Mrs. E. W. Ames.*

ORANGE PUDDING—No. 2.

One quart of milk, four eggs, one cup of sugar, three tablespoonfuls of corn starch, four large oranges. Heat the milk; beat the yolks of the eggs, sugar and corn starch together; stir into the milk while boiling, and cook until it begins to thicken. Slice the oranges, sprinkle over them a little sugar, and pour the custard over them. When cool, frost with the whites of the eggs.

Strawberries or peaches may be used instead of oranges.—*Miss Ella Moore.*

FIG PUDDING.

One-half pound of bread crumbs, one-half pound of figs, six ounces of brown sugar, two eggs, a little nutmeg, one-quarter pound of suet, a little milk, two ounces of flour; figs and suet chopped very fine and well mixed with the bread crumbs, flour, sugar and nutmeg. Add the eggs, well beaten, and the milk. Press the whole into a buttered mold, tie over it a thick cloth, and steam four hours. Serve with or without sauce.—*Mrs. Wm. Jeffers.*

PEACH PUDDING.

Slice one dozen peaches into a small pudding-dish, cover them with sugar and the following mixture: one egg, two-thirds of a cup of sugar, one-third of a cup of butter, one-half of a cup of milk, one and one-half cup of flour, one teaspoonful of cream of tartar, one-half teaspoonful of soda. Bake one hour, and serve with vanilla sauce. Apples may be used instead of peaches.—*Mrs. F. A. Brown.*

LEMON MERINGUE PUDDING.

One pint of milk, one-half pint of bread crumbs, yolks of two eggs, one-third of a cup of sugar, one lemon. After it is baked, add the whites of the eggs beaten to a stiff froth with two tablespoonfuls of sugar and a little of the lemon juice. Brown slightly in the oven.—*Mrs. S. F. Smith*, Newton Centre.

GINGER PUDDING.

Two cups of sugar, three cups of flour, three eggs, butter the size of two eggs, one cup of milk, two tablespoonfuls of ginger, one teaspoonful of cream of tartar, one-half teaspoonful of soda. Bake half or three-quarters of an hour and eat with sweet sauce.—*Mrs. J. H. Duncan.*

TAPIOCA FRUIT PUDDING.

One cup of tapioca in enough water to cover it. Boil, and as it thickens, add more water. When cooked, let it cool a little; sugar to taste. If berries are used, sweeten quite sweet, then mix with the tapioca and serve cold with cream and sugar. Peaches are especially delicious.—*Mrs. H. C. Graves.*

APPLE TAPIOCA PUDDING.

Take six large, tart apples, pare, quarter and core. Put in a dish and pour over them a cupful of tapioca soaked over night in a pint and a half of water, a cupful of sugar; flavor to taste. Bake about an hour, or steam. Serve with a rich sauce, or cream and sugar.—*Mrs. Martha C. How.*

APPLE DUMPLINGS.

One pint of flour, teaspoonful of cream of tartar, half a teaspoonful of soda, a little butter, mixed soft with milk. Pare and core six nice, large apples. Wrap each apple in a piece of crust. Bake more slowly than biscuit. Serve with sweet sauce.

FRUIT ROLL-UP

A rich cream of tartar biscuit made of a pint of flour; roll in an oblong form, spread with jelly, chopped apples, or any kind of berries; roll up; steam an hour. Serve with sweet sauce.

RHUBARB DUMPLINGS.

Crust like the last rule. Stir in half a pint of rhubarb cut in small pieces. Steam an hour and a half. Serve with sweet sauce. Very nice with cranberries instead of rhubarb.—*Mrs. C. R. Evans.*

CHERRY PUDDING.

Put three pints of cherries into a deep dish and cover with a crust made of rich biscuit dough. Set on the top of the stove and cover with a larger pudding-dish. Let it cook thirty-five minutes. This is equally good made with apples. Serve with hot or cold sauce.—*Mrs. E. G. Wood.*

SPANISH CHARLOTTE.

Place crumbs of stale bread or rolled crackers on the bottom of a pudding-dish, and put a layer of any kind of fruit or jelly over them. Continue alternately till the dish is nearly full, making the crumbs form the top. Pour a custard over it, and bake. Serve with sauce.—*Mrs. E. G. Wood.*

LEMON RICE PUDDING.

One cup of boiled rice, one pint of milk, grated rind of a lemon, butter the size of an egg, yolks of three eggs. Bake twenty minutes. Beat the whites of the eggs with half a pound of sugar, add the juice of the lemon, spread over the top of the pudding and brown lightly.—*Mrs. M. Steele.*

PLAIN RICE PUDDING.

Put a large half-cup of uncooked rice into a quart of milk, and add two-thirds of a cup of sugar, a little salt and butter. Bake about two hours. Frost if you please.—*T.*

PUFF PUDDING.

Three eggs, nine tablespoonfuls of flour, one pint of milk and a little salt. Pour the milk, scalding hot, on to the flour, stirring carefully to prevent any lumps. When cool, add the eggs, well beaten. Bake in a quick oven twenty or thirty minutes. Serve hot with liquid sauce.—*Mrs. C. C. Tyler*, Worcester.

CORN STARCH HASTY PUDDING.

One quart of milk, heated to scalding in a farina kettle. Wet with a little cold milk, four tablespoonfuls of corn starch and a teaspoonful of salt. Stir into the milk and let it boil ten minutes. Add a good lump of butter, and let the pudding stand without boiling in hot water for three minutes before serving.

SAUCE.

Two eggs, one cup of sugar, one-half cup of boiling milk. Flavor to taste. Beat the yolks and sugar together very light; pour into the boiling milk. Let it set in very hot, but not boiling water, stirring occasionally until just before serving, when beat in lightly the frothed whites. Or, one may serve with a sauce of sugar and water boiled together and a strong flavoring of vanilla.—*Mrs. E. W. Ames.*

GIPSY PUDDING.

Cut stale cake into thin slices, spread them with jelly or preserves. Place them in a deep glass dish. Pour over a hot, soft custard. Cool before serving. Or, cover the cake with whipped cream.

HASTY PUDDING.

Mix smooth a cupful of Indian meal and a teaspoonful of salt, in a little cold water. Stir it into a quart of boiling water. Continue to boil for half an hour, stirring often. If you wish to fry it, pour it hot into a pan which has been wet with cold water. When cold cut into slices, flour each side, and fry crisp and brown.

PUDDING SAUCE.

The traditional flavoring for pudding sauce is, of course, wine, but many of those who will use this book, believe with the Apostle Paul, that "it is good neither to drink wine nor anything whereby a brother stumbleth or is made weak." Of course the taste of the family must be consulted in providing a substitute. Vanilla, rose-water, lemon, vinegar, nutmeg and many other flavors are good.

No. 1.

One cup of powdered sugar, one-third of a cup of butter beaten to a cream, one egg beaten to a froth, one cup of boiling water. Add the juice of a lemon, and any other flavoring you like.—*Mrs. J. F. Davis.*

No. 2.

One egg, well beaten, and a scant cup of sugar. Beat them well together, pour over two-thirds of a cup of boiling milk. Flavor as you please.—*Mrs. J. A. Hale.*

No. 3.

One cup of water, one of sugar, (brown is best,) three teaspoonfuls of flour. Boil the sugar and water; wet the flour with water or milk, and stir till perfectly smooth; add it to the boiling mixture. Let this boil until clear, then add butter and any flavoring you please—a little vinegar is good. It must not be boiled after the butter is added.—*Mrs. L. Whittier.*

No. 4.

Beat the white of an egg very light, as for frosting; squeeze into it the juice of a lemon; add sugar to make it sufficiently sweet. Be careful to observe this order of mixing.—*Miss R. W. Duncan.*

No. 5.

Cream one-half cup of butter, until very light, add and beat with it one heaping cup of sugar. Just before serving add three or four tablespoonfuls of boiling milk, stirring briskly.—*Mrs. M. A. S.*

No. 6.—HARD.

One cup of sugar, one-fourth cup of butter rubbed to a cream. Add lemon juice and grated nutmeg.—*Mrs. J. F. Davis.*

No. 7.—HARD.

One-half cup of butter, one cup of powdered sugar, the grated rind and juice of half a lemon. Cream the butter thoroughly, and add the sugar gradually, beating hard and fast until it is very light. Add the lemon, and beat three minutes more. To be served *piled*, as it falls from the spoon—not smoothed.—*Miss Jennie Raymond.*

DESSERTS.

"A joint of mutton, and any pretty little tiny kickshaw, tell William cook."

SHAKSPERE.

ICE CREAM—No. 1.

Take a pint of milk, and when near the boiling point thicken it by stirring in the whites of two well-beaten eggs. Sweeten and flavor to taste. When cool, add a pint of cream. Freeze.—*Mrs. J. R. Nichols.*

ICE CREAM—No. 2.

One gallon of milk, sixteen eggs, one quart of cream, one-half pound of sugar to each quart, and flavor as you like. Put one-half of the milk in a pail and set it in a kettle of boiling water. Beat the eggs thoroughly, add the sugar, and when the milk is boiling hot, stir in the eggs and sugar, and stir continually until about the consistency of cream; then pour into a dish and add the cold milk and cream. Flavor when cold.—*Mrs. Helen A. Chase.*

ICE CREAM—No. 3.

One generous pint of milk, one cupful of sugar, half a small cupful of flour, two eggs. Let the milk come to boil. Beat the eggs, sugar and flour together and stir into the boiling milk. Boil twenty minutes, stirring often. Scrape one square of Baker's chocolate, and add to it two tablespoonfuls of sugar and one of boiling water. Stir this over the fire until smooth and glossy, and add it to the boiling mixture. Set it away to cool, stirring occasionally. When cold, add one teacupful of sugar and one quart of cream, and freeze. A teaspoonful of vanilla improves it.—*Miss Jennie Raymond.*

BAVARIAN CREAM.

Whip a pint of cream to a stiff froth. Boil another pint of cream or milk, with two tablespoonfuls of sugar, and flavor with vanilla, chocolate, strawberry or almond. When taken from the fire, add half a box of gelatine which has been standing for half an hour in cold water, near the stove. When slightly cool, stir in the yolks of four eggs, well beaten. When it has become quite cold and begins to thicken, stir for a few minutes until it is entirely smooth, then add the whipped cream lightly, until it is well mixed. Pour it into molds and place upon ice.—*Mrs. J. A. Hale.*

QUEEN'S CREAM.

One-half box of gelatine dissolved in a large cup of milk fifteen minutes, one quart of cream or milk, nine eggs, one large cup of sugar, one tablespoonful of vanilla. Heat cream or milk to almost boiling point, add gelatine, stir until dissolved, then add yolks of eggs and sugar, which must be well beaten together. Remove from the fire as soon as the custard thickens, and gradually stir in the whites—which must be beaten until you can turn the dish upside down. Pour into molds.—*Lizzie Ryan.*

PINK CREAM.

Three gills of raspberry syrup mixed with a quarter of a pound of powdered sugar and one pint of thick cream. Whisk until very light, and serve in whip glasses.—*Miss A. G. Beckwith*, Providence.

ROCK CREAM.

Boil one teacupful of rice in milk until very soft, sweeten with powdered sugar, pile on a dish, and when cold lay over it lumps of jelly, or preserved fruit of any kind. Beat whites of three eggs to a stiff froth, add a little sugar, flavor as you please, and pour over the rice.—*Mrs. M. L. Stover.*

ORANGE FLOATS.

One pint of cold water, one cup of granulated sugar, two lemons, (juice and pulp); let sugar and water come to boil, add lemon juice. Cut two oranges in slices, lay them in the bottom of a dish. Pour the lemon, when cool, over the oranges. Whites of two eggs beaten to a stiff froth for the top.—*S. C. G.*

CREAMED BANANAS.

Slice the bananas and strew them with sugar. Whip a cupful of cream very light. Whip the white of an egg to a stiff froth. Put them together, with a tablespoonful of sugar, and pour over the bananas. Peaches may be served in the same way.—*Mrs. F. A. Brown.*

VELVET CREAM.

Put one-half box of gelatine in one quart of cold milk, on the stove. When boiling, stir in yolks of three eggs, well beaten with six tablespoonfuls of sugar. Stir till it thickens to a custard, flavor, and when cold add the whites of the eggs beaten to a stiff froth. Pour into molds.—*Mrs. E. W. Ames.*

TAPIOCA CREAM.

Cover three tablespoonfuls of tapioca with cold water, and let it stand three hours, or over night. Stir it into a quart of boiling milk; add the yolks of three eggs, two-thirds of a cup of sugar, salt, and stir until it becomes a custard. Pour into a pudding-dish, cover with a frosting made of the whites of the eggs, brown in the oven.—*Mrs. Phineas How.*

BROWN CUSTARD.

Into a tin dish put two tablespoonfuls of sugar, let it slowly dissolve, then burn it, and pour upon it a pint of boiling milk, very slowly, as it will foam. Pour this mixture upon the eggs and sugar beaten together, (two yolks and white of one, with two tablespoonfuls of sugar.) Return it to the stove and let it come to boil. Just before serving, beat the whites of two eggs to a stiff froth and place on the top.—*Mrs. T. G. Appleton.*

CHOCOLATE CUSTARDS.

One pint of milk, three eggs, (yolks and whites separate,) one-half cup of sugar, two tablespoonfuls of grated chocolate, one teaspoonful of vanilla. Scald the milk and dissolve the chocolate in it. Put in the beaten yolks and sugar. Stir a minute before flavoring. Pour into the cups, which should be set in a pan of boiling water. Bake slowly about twenty minutes. When cool, place upon the top the beaten whites with powdered sugar.—*Mrs. J. D. Newcomb.*

SNOW PUDDING—No. 1.

Three tablespoonfuls of corn starch dissolved in a little cold water. Pour one pint of boiling water upon it; add salt, dessert-spoonful of sugar, juice of half a lemon, and the whites of three eggs beaten to a stiff froth; stir well; set in a basin of boiling water and scald ten minutes. Pour into cups and set away to form. Make a custard for it of a large half-pint of milk, scalded, with yolks of the eggs, sugar and salt. When ready to serve, pour the cups of snow pudding on to a platter; take out a spoonful from each and fill the cavity with jelly. Pour around it the custard.—*Mrs. Dr. Towle.*

SNOW PUDDING—No. 2.

Upon half a box of gelatine pour half a pint of cold water; let it stand a while, and then add one-half pint of boiling water. When cool, strain, and add the juice of two lemons, two cups of sugar, and whites of three eggs. Beat all together to a stiff froth, and pour into a mold. When ready to serve, pour over it a soft custard made with a pint of milk, the yolks of the eggs, and one more egg.—*Miss S. P. Whittier.*

CHARLOTTE RUSSE—No. 1.

Take one pint of cream, one tablespoonful of vanilla, one cup of sugar, and beat them to a froth. Add a quarter of a box of gelatine dissolved in as little water as possible—first in cold, then in hot. Add the whites of five eggs beaten to a stiff froth, and stir till it is well mixed. Pour the mixture into a dish lined with slices of sponge cake, and set it on the ice. Turn it out upon a platter and cover the top with another slice of sponge cake, when ready for the table.—*Mrs. J. A. Hale.*

CHARLOTTE RUSSE—No. 2.

One-half box of gelatine, soaked in a little cold water; one cup of milk. While boiling, add the gelatine and one cup of sugar. When cool, add one pint of cream, beaten light. Flavor with almond or vanilla. Line the dish with sponge cake cut in strips, fill with the mixture and set away to cool.—*Miss J. F. Smiley.*

CHARLOTTE RUSSE—No. 3.

One pint of cream beaten stiff, half a box of gelatine dissolved in half a pint of milk, the whites of two eggs well beaten, two cups of sugar, two teaspoonfuls of vanilla. First beat the cream. When stiff, pour on gelatine, eggs and sugar, quickly; stir well together. Have the dish lined with sponge cake, and pour in the mixture. Keep the cream as cool as possible while beating. Make a jelly of the other half box of gelatine; flavor as you please. When it is formed, garnish with it the top of the cream.—*Miss A. B. Train*, Newton Centre.

TAPIOCA ICE.

One cup of tapioca soaked over night. In the morning put it on the stove, and when it begins to boil put in a large cup of sugar, and boil until it is clear. Clear a good-sized pineapple free from all specks and chop it fine. Pour the tapioca boiling hot over the pineapple, and stir together. The hot tapioca will sufficiently soften the pineapple. Pour into moulds, and when cold eat with cream and sugar. Boil the tapioca in an earthen vessel to make it white.—*Miss Mary E. Webster*, Bradford.

COFFEE GELATINE.

One box of gelatine soaked two hours in one pint of cold water, two-thirds of a custard-cup of coffee, steamed in one pint of water, as for breakfast; one pint of sugar. Strain the coffee on the gelatine; add the sugar, with one pint and a half of boiling water. Place on the stove and let boil up once. Shape in moulds and set away to cool. Serve with cream and sugar.—*Mrs. S. D. Maynard.*

APPLE SNOW.

Beat the whites of three eggs to a stiff froth, add gradually a cupful of steamed apples and one of sugar. Make a boiled custard of the yolks of the eggs, one whole one, and a pint of milk. Serve with the apple.—*Mrs. H. Sawyer.*

QUINCE SAGO.

To one quart of water add six tablespoonfuls of sago. After soaking two hours, boil to a jelly, add a tumbler of quince jelly, put into a mould, and serve cold with cream.—*Miss A. G. Beckwith*, Providence.

GELATINE BLANC MANGE.

To one quart of milk, one-quarter of a box of gelatine. Soak the gelatine in a little of the cold milk, and when the rest of the milk is about boiling, add the gelatine with a little salt. Sticks of cinnamon are good boiled in the milk. One egg will improve it.—*Mrs. S. F. Smith*, Newton Centre.

APPLE SOUFFLE.

Bake four sour apples; sweeten the pulp and let it cool. Beat the white of one egg to a stiff froth, add the apple and beat together until very light.—*Miss A. E. Johnson*, Bradford.

MOONSHINE.

Beat the whites of six eggs to a siff froth. Add gradually six tablespoonfuls of pulverized sugar. Beat in a heaping tablespoonful of canned peaches or a cup of jelly. In serving pour in each saucer some cream, sweetened and flavored with vanilla, and on the cream place a portion of moonshine.—*Mrs. Dr. Cheney.*

DUTCH DANDY.

One quart of milk, three even tablespoonfuls each of flour and sugar, one dessertspoonful of vanilla, three eggs, a little salt. Put all but a small teacup of the milk in a pail, placed in scalding water. Smooth the flour in the teacupful of milk, and stir it carefully into the scalding milk, until well cooked; beat the sugar and vanilla with the yolks of the eggs and stir in, giving it just a scald. Pour into the dish for the table. Whip the whites of the eggs stiff, sweeten.

flavor with vanilla, and cover the dish with this frosting. Cut into squares or diamonds with a knife, and place in the hot oven just long enough to brown. Cool and put upon ice.—*Mrs. Wm. S. Karr, Hartford.*

STRAWBERRY CUSTARD.

Make a nice boiled custard of a quart of milk and the yolks of five eggs properly sweetened. Take a gill of sugar and a pint of ripe strawberries; crush them together and pass through a fine strainer. Take the whites of four of the eggs, and while beating them to a stiff froth add a gill of sugar, a little at a time. To the sugar and egg add the sweetened strawberry juice, beating all the while to keep it stiff. This makes a beautiful pink float, which is to be placed on top of the custard.

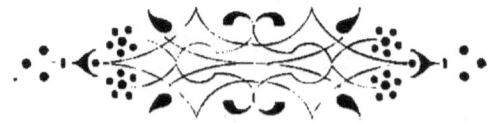

"A few strong instincts and a few plain rules."—WORDSWORTH.

In all cake-making, the first thing is to cream the butter and add the sugar, beating them well together. In most varieties it is best to separate the whites from the yolks of the eggs, and beat them to a very stiff froth. If the eggs are cold, this is very quickly accomplished; therefore keep them in a bath of cold water the night before using.

Cream of tartar and soda should be sifted together in the flour, and stirred in lightly just before the cake goes to the oven. If fruit is used, it should be added last of all.

The heat of the oven should be regular and even, and for thin cakes rather quick. In many ovens it is well to put a cold slide on the grate over the cake until it is risen, but in removing it do not admit any more air into the oven than is necessary. If it is desirable to move the cake, do it very gently, lest it fall.

When it is done it will settle a little away from the sides of the pan, or it may be tried with a clean broom straw. If it comes out dry, it is baked sufficiently.

WEDDING CAKE. 1817.

Twelve pounds of flour, twelve pounds of sugar, twelve pounds of currants, nine pounds of butter, five dozen eggs, two pounds of citron, one ounce each of cloves, cinnamon, mace, ginger, lemon peel, two ounces of nutmegs, one pint of brandy.

Frosting for the same: Four pounds of loaf sugar, the whites of ten eggs, half a pound of starch, one ounce of gum-arabic, lemon-juice and rose-water to flavor. This quantity will make three large loaves.—*Miss Caroline Duncan.*

WEDDING CAKE.

Two pounds butter, two pounds sugar, two pounds eleven ounces flour, six pounds currants, one and one-half pound raisins, one and one half pound citron, fourteen eggs, one-half ounce each of clove, cinnamon, nutmeg, mace, one and one-third teaspoonful of soda. Use two and one-half tumblers mixing, consisting of one-fourth tumbler of milk, one-fourth tumbler of molasses, and two tumblers of wine and brandy, or all wine. Two loaves.—*Mrs. M. Steele.*

BRIDE'S CAKE—No. 1.

One pound of butter, one and one-half pound of sugar, one and one-half pound of flour, one pint of whites of eggs, one pound of almonds—blanch and chop them very fine.—*Mrs. Sarah L. Holt.*

BRIDE'S CAKE—No. 2.

One-half cup of butter, one-half cup of corn starch, one-half cup of milk, one and one-half cup of sugar, one and three-fourths cup of flour, one teaspoonful of cream of tartar, one-half teaspoonful of soda, flavor to taste.—*Mrs. J. V. Smiley.*

POUND CAKE.

One-half pound of butter, fourteen ounces of sugar, fifteen ounces of flour, six eggs, one-half tumbler of milk, two-thirds teaspoonful of soda. Beat the butter and sugar to a froth, add the eggs, well-beaten, then the milk with the soda dissolved in it, and last the flour well stirred in. This makes two sheets.—*Mrs. Sarah L. Holt.*

ROYAL FRUIT CAKE.

Five cups of flour, five eggs, one and one-half cup of sugar, one and one-half cup of butter, one cup of molasses, small teaspoonful of soda, half a cup of milk, two pounds of chopped raisins, two of currants, half a pound of citron, one tablespoonful of cassia, one nutmeg, two teaspoonfuls of allspice and cloves. Less fruit and spice will be preferred by some. Bake slowly two hours. Cake made from this rule will be nicer at the end of a year than when first made.—*Mrs. J. D. Newcomb.*

FRUIT CAKE.

Three-fourths of a pound of sugar, three-fourths of a pound of butter, one pound of flour, two pounds of currants, one-half of a pound each of citron and raisins, six eggs, spice to taste, half cup of molasses, half teaspoonful of soda.—*Mrs. F. A. Brown.*

SPICE CAKE.

One cup of butter, half cup of sugar, half cup of molasses, two cups of flour, one teaspoonful of soda, half cup of sour milk, two eggs, one teaspoonful of every kind of spice, a cup of stoned and chopped raisins.—*Mrs. Wm. Smiley.*

RAISED CAKE—No. 1.

One cup of butter, two of sugar, one egg, half a pint of milk, one gill of yeast, five cups of flour. Raisins and spice to taste.—*Mrs. Rebecca Hale.*

RAISED CAKE—No. 2.

To a teaspoonful of soda, dissolved in hot water, add one-third of a cup of milk, and work with the hands into two cups of very light dough. Two eggs, two cups of sugar, large half-cup of butter, two cups of flour, spice and raisins. Bake in a deep pan.—*Mrs. C. W. Train.*

RAISED CAKE—No. 3.

One pound of butter, two of sugar, three of flour, one of chopped raisins, one of currants, cup of yeast, teaspoonful of soda. Spice highly. Mix with milk. Raise until very light. Bake in moderate oven. This quantity makes two loaves.—*Mrs. J. C. Green.*

SPONGE CAKE—No. 1.

Seven eggs, weight of six in sugar, weight of three in flour, salt, rind and juice of a lemon, a pinch of soda. The last thing, stir in the flour as lightly as possible. Bake in a sponge cake pan.—*Mrs. F. M. Sabine,* Bangor.

SPONGE CAKE—No. 2.

One and one-fourth cup of sugar, three eggs, two cups of flour, one teaspoonful soda, two of cream of tartar, one-half cup of water added the last thing. Whites and yolks of the eggs beaten separately. Soda and cream of tartar to be sifted two or three times in the flour.—*Mrs. H. C. Graves.*

SPONGE CAKE—No. 3.

Five eggs, one cup of sugar, one of flour, one teaspoonful of cream of tartar, (or better, the juice of a lemon,) half-teaspoonful of soda.—*Mrs. Martha A. Whittier.*

SPONGE CAKE—No. 4.

Six eggs, beat two minutes; three cups of sugar, beat five minutes; two cups of flour, two teaspoonfuls cream of tartar, beat two minutes; one cup of cold water, one teaspoonful soda, beat one minute; grated rind and juice of half a lemon, little salt, two more cups of flour, beat one minute. Observe the time exactly. Bake twenty minutes in a quick oven.—*Mrs. Jonathan Kimball.*

SPONGE CAKE—No. 5.

One coffee-cup of sugar, six eggs broken into the sugar and beaten twenty minutes, then stir in lightly one coffee-cup of flour. Bake three-fourths of an hour.—*Mrs. L. W. Johnson.*

SPONGE CAKE—No. 6.

Twelve eggs, the weight of ten in sugar, and of six in flour, juice and rind of one lemon. Beat the yolks well, add sugar and lemon, whites beaten to a stiff froth, and flour.— *Anne Stoddard,* Providence.

WHITE SPONGE CAKE.

Beat the whites of five eggs to a stiff froth, add a heaping tumbler of sugar and beat again about five minutes, (the sugar should be granulated and pulverized in equal parts,) a little salt. Stir in an even tumbler of flour—if Haxall is used, it should be a little scant. Lastly, add the juice of half a lemon. Bake in a deep round tin. Frost if you like.—*Mrs J. B. Tewksbury,* Bradford.

ANGEL CAKE.

Beat the whites of eleven eggs to a stiff froth; take an even cup of unsifted flour and sift it five times, to make it very light; add a cup of powdered sugar, and sift once with the flour, then add a half-teaspoon of cream of tartar and sift with the sugar and flour; pour in the eggs, and beat well together; add one teaspoonful of lemon or vanilla. Pour in angel-cake-pan and bake thirty minutes in a moderate oven. Do not butter the pan. Lay a cloth on your table, turn the pan upside down on it, when the cake is baked, and it will steam and fall upon the cloth in a few minutes.—*Mrs. W. R. Whittier.*

NUT CAKE—No. 1.

One cup of sugar, half cup of butter, half cup of milk, two cups of flour, teaspoonful of cream of tartar, half a teaspoonful of soda, two eggs, and one cup of nuts.—*Miss A. Hobbs.*

NUT CAKE—No. 2.

One cup sugar, one-half cup butter, one-half cup milk, two cups flour, two eggs, one coffee-cup chopped raisins, one of chopped English walnuts, teaspoonful cream of tartar, half teaspoonful soda. Beat butter to a cream, add sugar gradually, and when light, the eggs, well beaten, then the milk, then the flour, in which soda and cream of tartar have been mixed. Mix quickly; add raisins and nuts. Bake in a deep pan, in a moderate oven.—*Mrs. M. L. Stover.*

ENGLISH WALNUT CAKE.

One and one-half cup of sugar, half-cup of butter, two-thirds cup of milk, four eggs, (leaving out the whites of two for frosting,) two cups of flour, two teaspoons of cream of tartar, and one of soda, one pound of walnuts—leaving out twelve whole ones for top of cake. Break up the remainder and put in the cake.—*Mrs. Dr. Cheney.*

DOLLY VARDEN CAKE—No. 1.

Four eggs, yolks and whites beaten separately; two and one-half cups of sugar, one of butter, one of milk, four of flour, one-half teaspoonful of soda, one teaspoonful of cream of tartar. Divide the mixture into two parts, and to one part add one tablespoonful of molasses, one teaspoonful each of all kinds of spice, citron, currants, and raisins. Bake in loaves, first a layer of the light, then a layer of the dark.—*Miss A. C. Moulton.*

DOLLY VARDEN CAKE—No. 2.

Two cups of sugar, two-thirds of a cup of butter, two eggs, one cup of sweet milk, one teaspoonful of cream of tartar, half as much soda, flavor with lemon. Bake two-thirds the above in two pans. To the remainder add one tablespoonful of molasses, one cup of chopped raisins, one-half cup of currants, citron chopped fine, one teaspoonful of all kinds of spice. When baked, put the cakes together with jelly.—*Mrs. W. F. Evans.*

UNION CAKE—No. 1.

One cup of butter, two of sugar, one of milk, three of flour, one-half cup of corn starch, four eggs, two teaspoonfuls of cream of tartar, one of soda, essence of lemon. Beat the whites and yolks of the eggs separately.—*Mrs. Helen A. Chase.*

UNION CAKE—No. 2.

Four eggs, one cup of butter, two of sugar, one of sweet milk, three of flour, one teaspoonful of cream of tartar, one-half teaspoonful of soda dissolved in the milk. Divide this mixture into three parts, and bake two parts in pans of equal size. To the remainder add one tablespoonful of molasses, one cup of stoned and chopped raisins, one cup of currants, one-quarter pound of sliced citron, one teaspoonful each of clove and allspice, a little mace and nutmeg, and one spoonful of flour. Bake in same size of pan as the others. Put the sheets together while warm, with jelly.—*Mrs. J. V. Smiley.*

CHOCOLATE CAKE—No. 1.

One cup of butter, two of sugar, five eggs, leaving out the whites of two; one cup of milk, half a teaspoonful of soda, one teaspoonful of cream of tartar, three and a half cups of flour.

For the frosting, add to the whites of two eggs one and a half cup of sugar, (scant,) two teaspoonfuls of vanilla, and seven tablespoonfuls of grated chocolate.—*Miss M. F. Stuart.*

CHOCOLATE CAKE—No. 2.

One-half cup of milk, two and three-fourths cups of flour, one and one-half cup of sugar, one large cup of butter, one teaspoonful of vanilla, one of cream of tartar, half teaspoonful of soda, two and one-fourth squares of Baker's chocolate. Rub butter and sugar to a cream, then add four beaten eggs, saving two of the whites for frosting; next the chocolate, melted, and other ingredients.

For the frosting, use whites of two eggs, one and one-half cup of pulverized sugar. Mix well together, set on the fire, stir until it begins to simmer; take off, and beat until thick.—*Mrs. Amos Davis.*

CHOCOLATE CAKE—No. 3.

Half a cup of butter, two cups of sugar, three of flour, three eggs, one teaspoonful of cream of tartar, half teaspoonful of soda. Bake in Washington pie tins.

FILLING.

One cup of grated chocolate, one of water, one of sugar. Cook till it thickens. Put it between the layers and frost the top with chocolate frosting.—*Mrs. R. H. Ayer.*

CREAM CAKES.

Put half a pint of water and half a cup of butter on the stove, and when it boils stir in quickly two cups of dry flour. Then take from the stove, and when it is cool, stir in four eggs and a pinch of dry soda. Drop on buttered tins and bake in a quick oven. When cool, cut open and put in cream.

CREAM.

Stir into a pint of boiling milk, one egg, a cup of sugar and three-fourths of a cup of flour well beaten together.—*Mrs. S. Stuart.*

ÆSTHETIC CAKE.

One half cup of butter, two of flour, one of sugar, one half cup of milk, whites of two eggs, one half teaspoonful of soda and one teaspoonful of cream of tartar, flavor to taste. Make frosting from the yolks of the eggs.—*Mrs. Dr. Wm. Sellers.*

WATERMELON CAKE.

Four eggs, yolks and whites beaten separately; two cups of sugar, one of milk, one of butter, one teaspoon of cream of tartar, half a teaspoon of soda, three and a half cups of flour—possibly a little more. When well mixed, take out half and add to it a little red sugar, to color it, and a cupful of seedless raisins, to represent melon seeds. Put the white outside and the red in the centre. Two persons can fill the pan better than one.—*Mrs. C. N. Rhodes.*

ORANGE CAKE.

One cup of butter, two of sugar, one of milk, three and a half of flour, five eggs—leaving out the whites of three, one teaspoonful of cream of tartar, half teaspoonful of soda, and grated peel of two oranges. Bake in jelly-cake pans. For the frosting, beat the whites of three eggs to a stiff froth, add half a pound of powdered sugar and the juice of the oranges. When the cake is cool, spread each one with the frosting, laying one upon the other.—*Miss J. F. Smiley.*

GOLD CAKE.

One-half cup of butter, one of sugar, two of flour, yolks of four eggs, one-half teaspoonful of soda, one scant teaspoonful of cream of tartar. Flavor with vanilla or nutmeg.

SILVER CAKE.

The same as last rule, using the whites instead of the yolks of the eggs, and flavoring with almond. In both, the eggs should be added the last thing.—*Mrs. A. L. George.*

BUTTER SPONGE CAKE.

Three eggs, one cup of sugar, one of flour, three tablespoonfuls of milk and three of melted butter, lemon, one teaspoonful of cream of tartar, half teaspoonful of soda.—*Mrs. Helen A. Chase.*

DATE CAKE.

One cup of butter, two of sugar, four of flour, two-thirds of a cup of milk, four eggs, one and one-half pound of common dates, stoned but not chopped; two teaspoonfuls of cream of tartar and one of soda. Makes two loaves.—*Mrs. Walter N. Dole*, Lynn.

CREAM CAKE.

Bake any kind of nice plain cake in jelly-cake tins. Sponge cake is very good. Take one cup of sweet cream, one tablespoon of sugar and a little lemon or vanilla. Beat to a stiff froth. Just before it is ready to change to butter, spread it between the cakes.—*Mrs. Wm. Fitz*, Providence, R. I.

JOHNSON CAKE.

One cup of butter, two of sugar, one of milk, three and a half of flour, one teaspoonful cream of tartar, half a teaspoonful of soda, five eggs—leaving out the whites of two. Frost with the whites of the two eggs and a half cup of sugar.—*Mrs. Dr. Crowell.*

ALMOND MACARONI.

One half pound of blanched almonds, pounded with one teaspoonful of essence of lemon till a smooth paste. Add an equal quantity of sifted white powdered sugar and the beaten white of an egg. Work well together with a spoon. Dip the hands in cold water and mould them the size of a nutmeg. Put them on white paper, two inches apart, and let them cook in a cool oven about three-quarters of an hour.—*Miss A. B. Train.*

COCOANUT PIE.

Yolks of six eggs, two cups of sugar, one of milk, large half cup of butter, three cups of flour, one teaspoonful of cream of tartar, half teaspoonful of soda. Bake in four round pans.

MIDDLE.

Whites of four eggs, four tablespoonfuls of desiccated cocoanut, sugar. Spread this between two cakes.

FROSTING.

Whites of two eggs and sugar for a soft frosting, then sprinkle cocoanut over it freely.—*Miss S. P. Whittier.*

GERMAN CAKES.

One cup of sugar, two tablespoonfuls of butter, one cup of flour, four eggs, one teaspoonful of Cleveland's superior baking powder. Bake in two cakes.

FILLING.

Whites of five eggs, fifteen tablespoonfuls of sugar; add cocoanut; spread between and on top of layers.—*Mrs. A. H. Strong.*

FIG CAKE.

One pound of nice figs boiled fifteen or twenty minutes in a little water, one cup of stoned raisins. Chop them fine together: add a coffee-cup of sugar and juice of a lemon. This mixture may be put between two thin cakes of almost any variety.—*Mrs. L. E. Whittier.*

APPLE JELLY CAKE.

Bake almost any variety of cake in thin sheets. Put two of them together with a jelly made by simmering together two large grated apples, one cup of sugar, one egg, grated rind and juice of one lemon.—*C. P. T.*

LEMON JELLY CAKE.

One cup of butter, one and one-half cup of sugar, four eggs, one-half cup of corn starch, one and a half cup of flour, one teaspoonful of cream of tartar, half teaspoonful of soda, flavor with lemon.

JELLY.

The juice and grated rind of one lemon, a tablespoonful of butter, one cup of sugar and one egg. Beat all together and boil two or three minutes.—*Miss Colby.*

CREAM PIE.

Three eggs and a scant cup of sugar, well beaten together; one heaping teaspoonful of Cleveland's superior baking powder in a heaping cupful of flour, one tablespoonful of water. Bake in a quick oven.

CREAM.

Two-thirds of a pint of milk, one tablespoonful of corn starch, sugar, salt and vanilla to taste.—*Mrs. E. H. Drew.*

WASHINGTON PIE.

One cup sugar, two eggs, one and one-half cup flour, four tablespoonfuls water, one-half teaspoonful soda, one teaspoonful cream of tartar.

CREAM.

Two cups milk, one cup sugar, two eggs, two tablespoonfuls flour. Fill while warm, and set in a cool place.—*Mrs. Freeman Q. Barrows.*

GINGER PUFFS.

One cup of molasses, one of sugar, one large half cup of butter, one egg, one scant cup of cold water, one teaspoonful each of ginger and cinnamon, one teaspoonful of soda, four cups of flour. Drop on tins, as you do cream cakes. Very nice to eat hot.—*Mrs. Walter N. Dole,* Lynn.

SPICED CAKE.

One cup of milk, one of butter, two of sugar, three of flour, four eggs, one teaspoonful of soda, two of cream of tartar, three-fourths of a nutmeg, two tablespoonfuls of cinnamon.—*Mrs. H. C. Graves.*

CITRON TUMBLER CAKE.

Three tumblers of white sugar, one of butter, one of sweet milk, five of flour, one of chopped citron, four eggs, and one teaspoonful of soda. Flavor with lemon.—*Mrs. J. F. Davis.*

LEMON CAKE.

One teacupful butter, three of powdered sugar; rub to a cream. The yolks of five eggs well beaten, one teaspoonful of soda dissolved in one teacupful of milk, juice and rind of one lemon, whites of five eggs beaten stiff. Sift in as lightly as possible four cups of flour. Bake and frost.—*Mrs. Rebecca Hale.*

BROOKLYN CAKE.

One and one half cup of sugar, whites of six eggs, half a cup of butter, one-half a teaspoonful of soda, one of cream of tartar, half a cup of corn starch, one and one-half cup of flour, flavor with lemon.—*Mrs. J. F. Davis.*

PATTEN CAKE.

Break two eggs into a cup and fill it with cream. One cup of sugar, cup and a half of flour, teaspoonful of cream of tartar, half teaspoonful of soda. Flavor with lemon.—*Mrs. J. C. Green.*

RICE FLOUR CAKE.

One cup of butter, two and one-half of sugar, three of rice flour, six eggs, rind and juice of one lemon.—*Mrs. E. N. Hill.*

RICE FLOUR GOLDEN CAKE.

One cup of butter, two of sugar, beaten to a cream; yolks of six eggs, two-thirds of a cup of milk, one teaspoonful of soda, two of cream of tartar, one cup of rice flour, two of common flour, and lastly the beaten whites.—*Mrs. J. A. Hale.*

TEMPERANCE CAKE.

One cup of cream, one of sugar, two of flour, three-fourths teaspoonful of soda, spice.—*Mrs. Dr. Crowell.*

PLAIN CAKE.

One egg, half a cup of butter, one cup of sugar, one of buttermilk, (sour milk is less successful,) one teaspoonful of soda, flavoring to taste. All the ingredients may be stirred together at once.—*Mrs. C. H. Carpenter*, Newton Centre.

ELECTION CAKE.

At noon make a sponge of a quart of milk, a cup of yeast, and one of flour. At night add three-fourths pound of butter, one pound and a quarter of sugar, and flour enough to make it as stiff as buns. Bake the next morning in loaves. Smear with white of egg and molasses while the cake is warm, and put it back in the oven for a minute.—*Mrs. Moses W. Putnam.*

BUNS.

At noon take one and a half cup of new milk, one-half cup each of yeast and sugar, a little salt, flour enough to make a good sponge. Let it rise until night, then add one-half cup each of butter and sugar, a little nutmeg, currants, one-half teaspoonful soda, extract lemon, flour enough to mould thoroughly. Let it rise until morning, make in form of buns and put in pans. Wipe tops with milk and molasses. Let them rise an hour before baking.—*Mrs. M. L. Stover.*

MOLASSES GINGERBREAD.

One egg, one-half even cup of sugar, one-half large cup of molasses, two-thirds cup of sour milk, scant teaspoonful of soda, two teaspoonfuls of ginger, one large tablespoonful of butter, pinch of salt, flour to make stiff as sponge cake.—*Mrs. S. S. Hunking.*

HARD MOLASSES GINGERBREAD.

One cup molasses, three-quarters cup sugar, half cup butter, half cup cold water, teaspoonful soda dissolved in water, ginger and spice to taste.—*Mrs. Rebecca Hale.*

AMMONIA CAKES.

One ounce of ammonia, pounded fine, dissolved in two cups of milk. Two cups of sugar, one-third cup of butter, flour enough to roll easily. Bake in a quick oven. Put sugar on top.—*Miss Carrie Priest.*

DROP CAKES.

Two cups of sugar, one-half cup of butter, one cup of milk, two eggs, two teaspoonfuls of cream of tartar, one of soda, flour to make a stiff batter. Drop on pan. Flavor to taste.—*Mrs. Wm. Perley.*

SOFT SUGAR GINGERBREAD—No. 1.

Beat to a cream one cup of butter and three of sugar. Add one cup of milk and two and one-half of flour, into which two teaspoonfuls of cream of tartar have been stirred. Break into this mixture, five eggs; add tablespoonful of ginger, two cups of flour, a teaspoonful of dissolved soda, and bake in two large pans.—*Mrs. J. C. Tyler.*

SOFT SUGAR GINGERBREAD—No. 2.

Two eggs, one-half cup butter, one cup sugar, one-half cup milk, two cups flour, one-half teaspoonful soda, one teaspoonful cream of tartar. Flavor with ginger or nutmeg; sprinkle powdered sugar over the top before baking. This gingerbread is quite soft and may be cut into squares before it is taken from the pan.—*Mrs. M. F. Johnson.*

WHITE MOUNTAIN GINGERBREAD.

One half cup each of sugar and molasses, one and one half cup flour—large measure, a piece of butter the size of an egg, one egg, one teaspoonful each of clove, cinnamon, and ginger, one teaspoonful soda dissolved in one half cup of hot coffee, half cup of chopped raisins if you like.—*Mrs. Freeman Q. Barrows.*

NEW YORK GINGERBREAD.

Four cups flour, two of sugar, one of butter, one of milk, four eggs, two teaspoonfuls ginger, a pinch of mustard, two teaspoonfuls cream of tartar, one of soda.—*Miss A. B. Train.*

HARD GINGERBREAD—No. 1.

Two and one-half pounds of flour, three-fourths of a pound of butter, five eggs, two teaspoonfuls of soda, ginger to taste. To be rolled thin and baked on tin sheets.—*Miss Peggy Duncan.*

HARD GINGERBREAD—No. 2.

One cup of butter, three of sugar, four eggs, half-cup of milk, scant half-teaspoonful of soda, ginger to taste, and flour to roll very thin.—*Miss Maria Beach*, Framingham.

HARD GINGERBREAD—No. 3.

Two cups of sugar, one of butter, one egg, one teaspoonful of ginger, three tablespoonfuls of milk, one teaspoonful of soda, flour enough to roll.—*Mrs. Samuel Chase.*

HARD GINGERBREAD—No. 4.

One cup sugar, half-cup butter, one egg, tablespoonful sweet milk, half-teaspoonful soda, teaspoonful vanilla, flour to roll and cut in shapes.—*Mrs. Isaac Morse.*

HARD GINGERBREAD—No. 5.

One pound of butter, two of flour, one of sugar, six eggs, two teaspoonfuls of soda dissolved in a very little milk, flavor with lemon. Do not stir in more than two-thirds of the flour—reserve the rest to roll with. Bake on tin sheets.—*Mrs. M. Steele.*

CRUMPETS.

One egg, one cup brown sugar, one-half cup butter, one cup

chopped raisins or currants, half-teaspoonful soda in a large spoonful of milk, flour to roll thin.—*Miss Mary W. Johnson.*

JUMBLES.

One cup of sugar, one-half cup of butter, one egg, half-teaspoonful of soda, spice to taste. Cut off enough for a jumble, roll it out in sugar, with your hand, and lay it round in the form of a ring.—*Mrs. Phineas Webster.*

SOFT COOKIES.

One cup of butter, two of sugar rubbed to a cream, three well-beaten eggs, one cup of milk, six of flour, one teaspoonful of soda, and one of cream of tartar.—*Mrs. W. F. Evans.*

GRAHAM GINGER SNAPS.

Two cups of molasses, two-thirds of a cup of butter, one tablespoonful of ginger, one teaspoonful of soda, flour to roll thin, using equal quantities of Graham and wheat flour. Bake in a quick oven.—*Mrs. A. H. Herring.*

COCOANUT COOKIES.

Two cups of sugar, three-fourths of a cup of butter, two cups of grated cocoanut which has been soaked in milk an hour, two eggs, one teaspoonful of soda, flour enough to roll thin. Bake in a hot oven.—*Miss A. G. Beckwith*, Providence.

HERMIT CAKE.

One cup of sugar, two-thirds cup of currants, one-half cup of butter, one teaspoonful each of cinnamon and clove, one nutmeg, a third of a cup of milk, flour to roll quite thin. Brush them over with cream and dust with sugar before baking.—*Mrs. Charles B. Emerson.*

VANILLA WAFERS.

Two-thirds cup of butter, one cup of sugar, one egg, one tablespoonful of vanilla, four tablespoonfuls of milk, one teaspoonful of cream of tartar, half as much soda, flour to roll.—*Mrs. Dr. Hovey,* Newton Centre.

SUGAR COOKIES AND GINGERBREAD.

One cup of butter, two of sugar, two eggs, one tablespoonful of milk, half a small teaspoonful of soda, flour to roll very thin for cookies. Add another spoonful of milk and ginger, use less flour, roll thicker and bake in bars for gingerbread.—*Mrs. Leonard Whittier.*

WITCHES.

Two eggs, one and one-half cup of sugar, half-cup of butter, one tablespoonful of milk, half-teaspoonful of soda, one teaspoonful of cinnamon, cloves and allspice. Fruit, if you like. Roll quite thin.—*Mrs. Helen A. Chase.*

MOLASSES SNAPS.

One cup of molasses, three-fourths cup of sugar, tablespoonful of ginger, teaspoonful each of clove and cinnamon, one-half cup of melted butter, two teaspoonfuls of soda. Roll very thin.—*Mrs. M. Giddings,* Bangor, Me.

SPICE CAKES—No. 1.

Ten ounces butter, one pound sugar, two pounds flour, six eggs, two teaspoonfuls soda dissolved in a little milk, all kinds of spice. Roll thin, cut round, wet the tops with white of egg, and sprinkle sugar over them.—*Mrs. Sarah L. Holt.*

SPICE CAKES—No. 2.

One cup butter, one of sugar, half-cup molasses, half-cup water, teaspoonful each of cinnamon, ginger, caraway seeds, coriander seeds, one nutmeg, one teaspoonful soda, flour to roll out.—*Miss H. A. Bradbury.*

HAMLETS.

Two eggs, one and one-half cup brown sugar, one cup raisins chopped fine, two-thirds cup shortening, one teaspoonful each of cinnamon, nutmeg and cloves, one teaspoonful of soda dissolved in two great-spoonfuls of milk. Mix stiff, and cut like cookies.—*Mrs. I. Brown.*

CHOCOLATE COOKIES.

Half a pound each of flour, corn starch, butter and sugar, quarter of a pound of chocolate, two eggs, two tablespoonfuls molasses, one teaspoonful of Cleveland's superior baking powder. Mix soft as can be rolled. It rolls more easily to mix some time before you wish to bake.—*Mrs. Rebecca Hale.*

GELATINE FROSTING.

Soak one teaspoonful of gelatine half an hour in one tablespoonful of cold water, dissolve in two tablespoonfuls of hot water, add one cup of powdered sugar, stir until smooth.—*Miss A. Hobbs.*

EGG FROSTING.

The white of an egg beaten to a stiff froth; add gradually a large half-cup of powdered sugar, flavor with lemon, spread over cake. Wet a knife in cold water and smooth the frosting.

"And still she slept an azure-lidded sleep,
In blanched linen, smooth and lavendered,
While he from forth the closet brought a heap
Of candied apples, quince and plum, and gourd
With jellies soother than the creamy curd,
And lucent syrups tinct' with cinnamon."

KEATS.

CANNING FRUIT.

The first requisite is perfect cans. Fill them half full of water, put on the rings, screw down the covers, and turn them upside down to see if they can be trusted.

To prevent cracking them with the hot fruit, let hot water stand in them a little while before using, and keep them in a pan of hot water while filling; or if one prefers to fill them at a table instead of standing over the stove, it may be done safely if the cans are placed upon a folded cloth wrung out of cold water. As the hot fruit is put into the jar, steam will generate around it and keep it from cracking.

The jars must be filled quickly, while the fruit is boiling hot, yet it is best to rest a second between each ladle-full, that the bubbles of air may have a chance to rise.

See that the jars are absolutely full, and immediately screw on the covers very tightly. As the fruit cools, the glass will contract, so they should be tightened again after a little interval.

Use just what sugar you need to make the fruit agreeable. It is the hermetical sealing and not the sugar which preserves the fruit.

The preserves should be kept in a dark place.

PEARS.

Steam the pears until soft. Take them from the steamer, sprinkle over the sugar, (half the weight of the fruit, or less.) When the sugar is dissolved, put them into a kettle and cook in the syrup about ten minutes. Can immediately.

PEACHES.

Pare. halve and stone them, or cook them whole, as you please. At least a few stones should be left in each can, for the sake of the flavor. Make a syrup of a cupful of sugar and a half-cupful of water for each quart can. Simmer the fruit in it until it is transparent. Shake the kettle frequently to prevent burning. Cook only enough for one jar at a time, and they will not break.

QUINCES.

Peel, halve, and carefully remove the whole of the core. Boil in a little water until tender. Use this water with one-half or three-fourths the weight of sugar to make the syrup. Skim thoroughly, add the quinces, and cook about twenty minutes.

STRAWBERRIES.

Use about one-third the weight of sugar. Put the sugar to the berries over night, or not, as you please, but do not use any water. The moisture of the berries will soon dissolve the sugar. Put all together in the kettle, cook until just scalded through, and can.

PINEAPPLE.

Grate the fruit, or cut it into small pieces. Mix the sugar with the fruit and let it stand over night. Drain off the syrup, boil and skim, add the fruit, let it boil slowly about twenty minutes, and can.

PLUMS.

Vary the quantity of sugar according to the variety of plum. Make the syrup with a little water and proceed as with other fruit.

CURRANT JELLY.

Pick over the fruit carefully, but neither wash nor remove from the stems. Press out the juice with a silver spoon, and strain it through a fine cloth. Allow a pound of sugar for each pint of juice. Put the sugar on flat pans and heat it in the oven, taking care not to let it brown. Stir the hot sugar into the strained juice, and when it is thoroughly dissolved, fill the jelly-tumblers. Let them stand in a sunny place for a few days. It is said that all kinds of jellies are much better if made on sunny days. Made by this recipe, the jelly preserves the taste of fresh currants.—*Mrs. Elbridge Wood.*

CURRANT JELLY—No. 2.

Take the currants when they are just ripe; if over-ripe, the jelly will not form. Mash and cook a little in their own juice, without water. Strain through a flannel bag. Take equal quantities of juice and sugar. Put the sugar into a very moderate oven to heat, but not brown. Put the juice over the fire and let it boil slowly, skimming as long as any scum rises. When clear, stir in the hot sugar and simmer about five minutes longer.

BARBERRY JELLY.

Take the fruit when ripe and plump, before the frost has touched it. To four quarts, picked from the stems, put a very little water, and stew until soft. Strain and proceed as in currant jelly, cooking a little longer after adding the sugar, if it seems to be necessary.

GRAPE JELLY.

Pick the grapes from the stems. To four quarts put about a pint and a half of water. Boil until quite soft; pour into a hair sieve; take the juice which *runs* through, and proceed as in the last rule for *jelly*.

Then *press* through all the pulp. To one quart of this add one pint of sugar, boil about ten minutes, and you have a nice *jam*, which may be canned for future use.

PRESERVED GRAPES.

Push the pulp from the skins. Cook it a little so that it can be freed from the seeds by rubbing through a sieve. Cover the skins with water and boil an hour, or longer if necessary to make them very tender. Put the skins and pulp together with an equal quantity of sugar. Simmer about twenty minutes longer.—*Mrs. B. F. Hosford.*

PRESERVED ORANGE PEEL.

Cut the peel of oranges into narrow shreds and boil until tender, changing the water three times. Use pound for pound of sugar and peel. Squeeze the juice of the oranges over the sugar. Boil twenty minutes all together.—*Mrs. A. N. Arnold.*

PRESERVED GREEN TOMATO.

Skin the tomatoes, and take three-fourths of a pound of brown sugar to one pound of tomatoes. Boil them to a jam, with ginger-root and slices of lemon; add a little vinegar, if you please.—*Mrs. Robert Harris,* New York.

PRESERVED CITRON.

Cut citron into thin rings, remove seeds and rind, cut into small pieces. Allow a pound of sugar to a pound of fruit. Put the sugar in a kettle with a little water—a gill or more to a pound, and stir until well dissolved. Place upon the stove and add sliced lemons, at the rate of a lemon to a pound, and if you please, some lumps of ginger-root. Let it boil one-half to three-quarters of an hour, then add the citron, and boil until tender.—*Mrs. Newton Stover,* Sedgwick, Me.

QUINCE MARMALADE.

Cores and parings of a peck of quinces, and six whole quinces cut up. Cover with water, boil till soft, sift through a sieve. To one bowl of quince add one bowl of sugar; boil together slowly for three or four hours. When it has become sufficiently thick, put into bowls or molds; or it may be spread on a platter an inch in depth. It will harden in a week or so, and may then be cut into squares to keep.—*Mrs. Mary Winchester,* Framingham.

QUINCE AND APPLE.

Equal quantities of quince and sour apples, both pared and quartered. Two quarts of sugar to three quarts of fruit. Partly cook the quinces, and then add the apples.—*Annie Stoddard,* Providence.

MOLASSES QUINCE.

Equal quantities of quince and sweet apples, (not pared,) with three-fourths the quantity of molasses. Cook all together until soft.—*Annie Stoddard,* Providence.

BUTTERED APPLES.

Two pounds of quartered apples, one-fourth pound of butter. Put the butter into a spider, then the quarters of apples, and sprinkle them with one-half pound of sugar. Put in a cool oven and let them roast slowly. Serve on toast with a sprinkling of sugar over them.—*Miss A. B. Train,* Newton Centre.

APPLE SAUCE.

Wash, quarter and core the apples, but do not pare them. Put as much sugar as they will need in a sauce-pan with a little water.

When it boils, add the apples and let them stew slowly, without stirring, until soft. Serve immediately.—*Mrs. C. W. Train.*

APPLE JAM.

Use equal quantities of brown sugar and sour apples. Make a syrup of the sugar, carefully removing the scum; add the apples, chopped, some grated lemon peel and a few lumps of white ginger. Simmer several hours, until the apple looks clear and yellow.

TO STEW CRANBERRIES.

One quart of cranberries, one pint of sugar, one-half pint of water. Put all together, and do not stir.—*Mrs. Margaret Longley.*

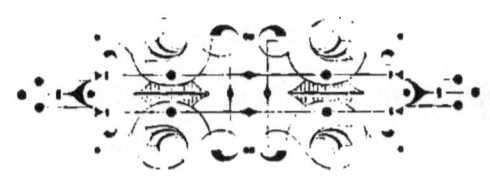

PICKLES.

"Sabean odors from the spicy shores of
Araby the blest."

MILTON.

CUCUMBERS.

Place a hundred small cucumbers and a pint-of salt in a jar and pour on them boiling water. Cover them closely for twenty-four hours, then take them from the jar and wipe each of them with a soft towel. Wash the jar and replace them, pouring on them scalded vinegar, with such spices as you please. These pickles will very soon be ready for use.—*Mrs. J. H. Duncan.*

MIXED PICKLES.

Take small cucumbers, onions, cauliflower, sliced cabbage, green tomatoes, parboiled and sliced carrots, peppers, beans, and grated or sliced horse radish. Let all excepting the horse radish remain in salt and water forty-eight hours. Drain thoroughly. To two gallons of vinegar add one-quarter of a pound each of turmeric powder and mustard, one tablespoonful of curry. Scald the vinegar, add the other ingredients, and pour hot over the cucumbers. Cover tight and keep in a cool place.—*Mrs. S. Stuart.*

PICCALILLI—No. 1.

Chop or slice one-half bushel of green tomatoes; sprinkle with salt; let them stand over night; in the morning drain them and cook in weak vinegar with one pound of green peppers. Put into a stone jar a layer of tomatoes, a layer of horse radish and sugar, and spice-bags of cinnamon, allspice and cloves; cover with strong vinegar.—*Mrs. E. H. Drew.*

PICCALILLI—No 2.

Slice one peck green tomatoes, add one cup of salt, let it stand till morning, drain off the water. Put them in a kettle over the fire and cover with vinegar. Add two cups white sugar, five chopped onions, five chopped peppers, two spoonfuls each of mustard and ginger, half-spoonful each of allspice and cinnamon.—*Mrs. Dr. Sellers.*

CAULIFLOWER PICKLE.

Boil the cauliflower—after stripping it into small pieces—in weak vinegar with a little salt, drain, and to one peck of cauliflower pour vinegar enough to cover it, after letting the vinegar come to the boiling point, with the following ingredients in it: one-half pound brown sugar, two ounces ground mustard, one ounce each of turmeric, celery seed, white mustard seed, ground pepper, and cloves. Less mustard may be used if this is too highly seasoned.—*Mrs. C. P.*

CHOW CHOW.

One peck of green tomatoes, three good-sized onions, six green peppers, seeds taken out. Chop and boil together with two quarts of vinegar; strain, and throw away the vinegar. Then to three quarts of new cider vinegar, scalding hot, add twelve pickled limes chopped fine, one cup of mixed mustard, one cup of sugar, three tablespoonfuls of salt, one dessertspoonful each of cloves, cinnamon and allspice, and pour hot over the tomatoes.—*Mrs. Walter N. Dole*, Lynn.

AMERICAN CAPERS.

Pick green nasturtion seeds fresh from the vines, cover them with vinegar, and just scald them.—*Mrs. Rebecca Hale.*

STUFFED PEPPERS.

One dozen peppers. Cut off the tops and remove the seeds and pulp, and soak in weak brine for twenty-four hours. Chop green tomatoes, red cabbage, onions and one pepper together, and fill the peppers with the mixture. Sew on the tops and pour over them boiling vinegar. They are very nice sliced.—*Mrs. H. S. Littlefield.*

RIPE CUCUMBER PICKLE.

Take large, ripe cucumbers, before the frost touches them. Pare and take out the seeds, chop—not very fine, add salt in the proportion of a spoonful to two quarts of cucumber. Let them stand over night. rinse well in cold water, and leave in colander till perfectly drained: then put into jars and add pepper and cold vinegar. They retain the flavor of fresh cucumbers.—*Mrs. Geo. W. Bosworth*, Cambridge.

PICKLED EGGS.

Boil eggs hard, take off the shells. Put the eggs in a jar and pour on them scalding vinegar flavored with ginger. pepper and allspice. Good with cold meats.—*Mrs. C. R. Evans.*

PICKLED PEARS.

Seven pounds of fruit, three of sugar, one ounce of whole cloves, one ounce of stick cinnamon, one pint of vinegar. Pare the fruit. When the sugar and vinegar boil, skim, and boil the fruit in it till it is soft. Place the pears in the jar while hot and sprinkle with the spice. Pour on the syrup while hot.—*Mrs. T. G. Appleton.*

PICKLED PEACHES.

Twelve pounds of peaches, six pounds of brown sugar, one pint of vinegar. If spice is desired, one-half stick of cinnamon and one-quarter ounce of whole cloves. Pour boiling water on the peaches and dry them with a cloth without breaking the skin. Simmer sugar and vinegar together, then put the fruit into the syrup and boil gently until cooked to the stone.—*Miss A. B. Train, Newton Centre.*

PICKLED BLACKBERRIES.

Three quarts berries, one pint vinegar, one pound sugar, cloves. Simmer two or three hours.—*Mrs. M. L. Stover.*

SPICED CURRANTS.

Five pounds of currants, four of sugar, one pint of vinegar, two tablespoonfuls each of clove and cinnamon. Cook three-fourths of an hour.—*Mrs. Dr. Crowell.*

PICKLED CHERRIES.

Seven pounds of fruit (white heart), four of sugar, one pint of vinegar, spices, cloves and cinnamon. Boil all together and can.—*Mrs. J. W. B. Clark.*

SPICED CHERRIES.

Six pounds of fruit, three of sugar, one pint of vinegar, cloves and cinnamon to suit the taste. Boil two hours. This will keep without being canned.—*Mrs. J. W. B. Clark.*

"A wilderness of sweets."—MILTON.

CLEAR CANDY.

Two cups white sugar, one of water, large teaspoonful of vinegar. Do not stir. Flavor to taste. Work this as molasses candy, or use it to candy nut meats, dropping them into the mixture. Take them out with two forks and put on marble to cool.—*Miss A. B. Train,* Newton Centre.

BUTTER TAFFY.

One cup of sugar, one-half cup of molasses, two tablespoonfuls of water, two of vinegar, butter size of an egg.—*Miss J. F. Smiley.*

CHOCOLATE CARAMELS.

One cup of grated chocolate, one of milk, one of molasses, one of sugar, butter size of an egg. Boil until it thickens, then cool in shallow pans.—*E. A.*

CHOCOLATE CREAMS.

Half cake Baker's chocolate, melted in a bowl over a kettle of boiling water; two cups sugar, in two and a half cups of milk or water. Boil hard five minutes, and flavor with vanilla. Stir until it becomes a paste, then roll into little balls with the hands. When hard, drop them into the melted chocolate; lift out with two forks; cool on marble or buttered dish.—*S.*

COCOANUT CANDY.

Six cups white sugar, three of grated cocoanut, three of water. (using the milk of the nut, if perfectly sweet, adding water to it to make the three cups.) Boil sugar and water until very thick, then add the cocoanut until as thick as pudding. Turn on to a platter or marble to cool, and cut in squares.—*B.*

WALNUT CREAM.

Two cups of sugar, two-thirds cup of milk, one-third pound of English walnuts. Boil seven minutes; take from the stove and beat to a cream, putting in the nuts when partially thickened; pour in a dish to cool.—*Miss M. F. Stuart.*

PEPPERMINTS.

One cup sugar (not granulated), one-quarter cup boiling water. Boil without stirring, seven minutes; beat until thick; add three or four drops of oil of peppermint. Drop quickly on paper. Checkerberry or grated chocolate may be used instead of peppermint.—*Miss Ellen Johnson*, Newton Centre.

MARSH MALLOW PASTE.

Dissolve one-half pound of gum Arabic in one pint of water; strain and add half a pound fine sugar and place over the fire, stirring constantly till the syrup is dissolved and all is the consistency of honey; add gradually the whites of four eggs, well beaten; stir the mixture till it becomes somewhat thin and does not adhere to the finger; pour all into a pan slightly dusted with powdered starch, and when cool divide into small squares. Flavor to the taste just before pouring out to cool.—*Mrs. J. P. Worstell.*

MOLASSES CANDY.

One cup sugar, two of molasses, tablespoonful of vinegar. Boil about twenty minutes, or until it hardens in cold water. Stir in a teaspoonful of dry soda, and pour into buttered tins; when cool, pull and cut in sticks.

MOLASSES CANDY—No. 2.

Boil Porto Rico molasses until it hardens in cold water; pour on buttered pans; when cool, work with the hands and pull until very white.—*Mrs. M. Steele.*

BEVERAGES.

Now clear the fire and close the shutters fast,
Let fall the curtains, wheel the sofa round,
And while the bubbling and loud-hissing urn
Throws up a steaming column, and the cups
That cheer but not inebriate, wait on each;
So let us welcome peaceful evening in.
COWPER.

Coffee, which makes the politician wise,
And see through all things with his half-closed eyes.
POPE.

TEA.

Use an earthen teapot. An even teaspoonful of tea is the usual allowance for one person. Scald the teapot, put in the tea, and add the needed amount of *boiling* water. Cover closely and let it steep five minutes, *not boil*. English Breakfast tea requires longer steeping, and some persons prefer it boiled for two or three minutes.

COFFEE—No. 1.

Mix an egg with the coffee, without beating; pour cold water over it, and let it boil up once or twice.—*Annie Stoddard.*

COFFEE—No. 2.

Save your egg-shells. Crumble one in a cup, pour on a little boiling water, and mix it with your coffee. Put it in the coffee-pot, add boiling water, and boil slowly about ten minutes.

CHOCOLATE.

Add to one ounce of chocolate, two tablespoonfuls of sugar and one of water. Stir in a small sauce-pan over the fire, until perfectly smooth and glossy. Stir this into one quart of boiling water, or milk and water. Mix thoroughly and serve immediately. Do not let it boil after adding the milk.—*Mrs. M. L. Stover.*

CRUST COFFEE.

Take a large crust of brown bread; dry it in the toaster, and at last almost burn both sides; lay it in a sauce-pan and pour boiling water on it; boil it a minute or two, then strain off the coffee. It should be strong enough to look like real coffee, of which it is a very good imitation when well made.

UNFERMENTED GRAPE WINE.

To one peck of grapes add two quarts of water. Thoroughly bruise the grapes and let them stand in the water over night; strain, and add seven pounds of sugar to a gallon; simmer over a slow fire and skim until it becomes clear; let it boil a little, taking care not to burn; strain into jars, and when cool, bottle for use. To be diluted with water the night before using.—*Mrs. C. N. Rhodes.*

ENGLISH GINGER BEER.

Pour four quarts of boiling water upon an ounce and a half of ginger, an ounce of cream of tartar, a pound of white sugar, and two fresh lemons, sliced thin. It should be raised twenty-four hours, with two gills of good yeast, and then bottled. It improves by keeping several weeks, unless the weather is hot, and is an excellent beverage.

LEMON POP.

Put one pound of brown sugar into a stone jar with one sliced lemon, one and one-half tablespoonful of ginger tied in a bag; add five quarts of boiling water. When lukewarm, add one-half pint of yeast; let it remain twelve hours, then bottle for use.—*Miss Grace C. Rhodes.*

MEAD—No. 1.

Five pounds of sugar, two quarts of cold water, white of one egg, quarter of a pound of tartaric acid, two ounces essence of sassafras, half-ounce essence of checkerberry. Stir the egg into the water, then put in the sugar, and let it boil; add one-half pint of water to stop its boiling. Let it boil again, add more water, skim, and let boil again; skim again; when cool, strain, add acid and essence, and bottle for summer drink.—*Mrs. O. D. Cheney.*

MEAD—No. 2.

Three and one-half pounds of brown sugar, one and one-half pint of molasses, two quarts boiling water, one-fourth of a pound of tartaric acid and one ounce of sassafras. Put sugar, molasses and tartaric acid into a jar, pour the boiling water over them; let stand over night; in the morning add the sassafras and bottle for use.—*Mrs. Wm. S. Perley.*

RASPBERRY VINEGAR.

Cover ripe raspberries with vinegar, and let them stand two or three days, then mash and strain. To a pint of juice add a pint of white sugar; boil twenty minutes, and skim; bottle when cool. A little of this in a glass of water is a very refreshing drink.

FOR THE SICK.

'Tis a little thing
To give a cup of water; yet its draught
Of cool refreshment, drained by fevered lips,
May give a shock of pleasure to the frame
More exquisite than when nectarean juice
Renews the life of joy in happiest hours.
HARTLEY COLERIDGE.

BEEF TEA—No. 1.

Take one pound of beef from the round, trim off all shreds and fat, and chop fine. Put in a bowl or porcelain-lined saucepan, and add one large cup of cold water; set on the range where it will warm very slowly; stir it constantly, and as soon as the juice begins to change color take it from the fire, and let it stand fifteen minutes: then wring through a strong crash towel. Add salt when it is wanted for use. One or two spoonfuls of this, given at intervals of an hour, to patients' who cannot take other food, will nourish the system, and is a better stimulant, in cases of debility, than brandy.—*Julia A. Marshall, M. D.*

BEEF TEA—No. 2.

Choose a lean and juicy piece of beef, the size of your hand; take off all the fat; broil it only three or four minutes, on very hot coals; lay it in a porringer or bowl, sprinkle it with salt, and pour upon it two or three gills of boiling water; then cut it into small pieces as it lies in the water. Cover it closely, and let it stand where it will keep hot, but not boil.

BEEF TEA—No. 3.

Cut a piece of lean, juicy beef into pieces an inch square, put them into a wide-mouthed bottle and cork it tight; set the bottle into a kettle of cold water and boil it an hour. This mode of making beef tea concentrates the nourishment more than any other.—*A. B. C.*

BEEF JUICE.

Heat a thick slice of beefsteak just enough to start the juice. (do not cook it); squeeze out all the juice with a lemon-squeezer; add a little salt.

OATMEAL GRUEL.

To one quart boiling water, gradually add one-half cup steam-cooked oatmeal. Boil it gently one-half hour. stirring frequently. If it boils away too much, add a little water. Strain thoroughly, salt and return to the stove. and add milk at pleasure, letting it *heat*, but not boil. Serve immediately.—*Mrs. M. L. Stover.*

ARROWROOT GRUEL.

Two tablespoonfuls of arrowroot, one pint each of sweet milk and boiling water; sweeten with loaf sugar.

GLUTEN GRUEL.

Into one quart of boiling water stir two tablespoonfuls of Gluten Flour, mixed thoroughly in cold water. Boil from fifteen to twenty minutes, season with salt, add sugar, milk or cream, if desired.

PLEASANT DRINK IN FEVER.

Put half a pint of dried sour apples into a quart pitcher, and fill it with boiling water. When cold it is ready to drink, either with or without ice. Fresh sour apples may be used in the same way.—*Mrs. M. C. How.*

DRINKS FOR THE SICK.

Pour boiling water upon mashed cranberries, apples, currants or raspberries; pour off the water, sweeten and cool.

Toast a crust of white bread very brown, without burning it, and put it into cold water. After an hour the water will be a refreshing drink.

Pour boiling water upon brown bread toasted quite brown, or upon pounded parched corn, boil a minute, strain, add sugar and cream or milk.—*T. C. W.*

TO PREPARE RAW EGG.

Beat the yolk and a teaspoonful of sugar in a glass; stir in a teaspoonful of wine, if it is needed, or flavor with nutmeg; add the white of the egg, beaten to a stiff froth. Eggs are very palatable served simply with a little iced water.—*T. C. W.*

SAGO CREAM FOR INVALIDS.

Boil one dessertspoonful of sago in a little water until it is reduced to a clear jelly, add one cup of thick, sweet cream, and boil again. Beat a fresh egg very light and pour the hot sago upon it; sweeten and spice to taste. To be eaten either warm or cold.—*Mrs. J. A. Hale.*

TAPIOCA JELLY.

Tapioca, two tablespoonfuls; cold water, one pint. Boil very gently for an hour, or until it is a clear jelly; add sugar, nutmeg and lemon-juice to the taste. In some cases of illness it is desirable to add a little wine or brandy. It is especially valuable in throat troubles.—*Mrs. E. W. Ames.*

CHICKEN FOR AN INVALID.

Choose a very tender chicken; cut out the breast, salt it, rub a bit of butter on it, and broil it on a bed of live coals, not too hot. Turn it frequently, that the outside be not burned; it will be more delicate than if cooked in any other way.—*T. C. W.*

MILK PORRIDGE.

One quart of boiling milk—or milk and water—two tablespoonfuls of Gluten Flour mixed with a little cold milk and half a teaspoonful of salt; stir into the milk, and boil fifteen or twenty minutes.

MOSS TEA.

Rinse in cold water a few pieces of Irish moss, place it in an earthen dish, cover with a pint of cold water, let it heat up very gradually till it comes to boil, add more water if needed, boil two or three minutes, strain upon the juice of one or two lemons, and sweeten to the taste.—*Miss S. P. Whittier.*

BREAD FROM SPECIAL DIABETIC FOOD.

Use about one-half teacup of yeast to one quart of water; stir in flour sufficient to make sponge somewhat thinner than that from ordinary flour; knead the dough only enough to form the loaf. This makes two loaves. Bake about one hour. *Raise this as you would other flours.* Gluten Flour can be used in the same way.

LAUNDRY.

"Gars auld claes look amaist as weel's the new."
BURNS.

———✳———

Before washing black and white, stone, slate or maroon-colored cotton goods, dip them in a solution of salt and water, made by dissolving two cupfuls of salt in ten quarts of cold water, and hang them in a shady place to dry. The salt sets the colors. When dry, wash in a light suds in the usual way. Calicoes and muslins do not require a hot suds; water moderately warm is best. Wash quickly, turn the wrong side out, and dry in the shade. A little salt in the rinsing water is an improvement. For starch, use a little white glue water, cool and clean. Always iron on the wrong side, with a moderately hot iron.

Blue, stone, slate and brown-colored articles may also be made to retain their color perfectly by adding sugar of lead to the water in which they are to be washed. Dissolve one ounce of sugar of lead in a pailful of hot water, stir carefully until it is thoroughly dissolved, and let the mixture cool. When about milk-warm, put in the articles and let them remain an hour. Hang up to dry before washing. The sugar of lead fixes the color permanently, so that treatment with it will not need to be repeated. Use this preparation with caution; sugar of lead is poisonous.

Fruit or wine stains can be removed from silk, woolen or cotton goods by sponging them gently with ammonia and alcohol—a teaspoonful of ammonia to a wineglass of alcohol. Finish with clear alcohol. The fumes of a lighted match will remove remnants of stains.

JAVALLE WATER.

For removing fruit, tea, or other stains: One-half pound chloride of lime dissolved in two quarts of boiling water and strained; add one pound sal-soda dissolved in two quarts of boiling water. Put away in a jug, and use when needed. When used, dilute a little and soak the spots in it fifteen minutes, or longer.—*Mrs. L. Whittier.*

BORAX SOAP.

Two ounces of borax, two quarts of water, one pound of hard soap. Boil until the soap is dissolved, then let it cool. Cut the soap into small pieces before putting into water.—*Mrs. C. R. Evans.*

BLUEING FOR CLOTHES.

Put one ounce of Prussian blue powder into a bottle containing one quart of soft water. Add a quarter of an ounce of powdered oxalic acid. One teaspoonful will be sufficient to use for a washing.—*Mrs. W. R. Whittier.*

GLOSS FOR STARCH.

Two ounces of fine white powdered gum Arabic. Put in a pitcher and pour over it a pint of boiling water. Cover it and let it stand over night; then pour from the dregs into a bottle; cork and keep for use. Add a tablespoonful to a pint of starch.—*Mrs. A. L. George.*

CLEANSING CREAM.

Two ounces of white castile soap, two ounces of ammonia, half an ounce of ether, half an ounce of spirits of wine. Let the druggist put the three last ingredients in a vial together. Cut the soap fine and dissolve in one-half pint of soft hot water; add two quarts of cold water; put all together in a bottle, cork it tight, and use as may be needed to remove spots from black dresses, carpets, &c.—*Miss Susan Johnson*, Brunswick, Me.

TO CLEANSE BLACK WOOLEN GOODS.

To cleanse black woolen goods, wash them in warm soap-suds, rinse in strong blueing water. Do not wring at all, but hang upon the line until the dripping is over, then press upon the wrong side.

, Or buy an ounce of California soap-bark, pour upon it a pint of boiling water; when cool, strain. Sponge the goods with it upon the right side, and press immediately upon the wrong side.

OXALIC ACID.

To remove ink-stains, iron-rust, etc., from *white* goods, use oxalic acid. Upon an ounce of the acid pour a pint of boiling water. Keep it in a bottle marked "POISON," away from the children. Wet with it the stained article, and hold it over the steam of hot water. Wash all the acid from the article, or it will injure the fabric.

MISCELLANEOUS.

"Here's to the housewife that's thrifty."
SHERIDAN.

FOR CLEANING SILVER.

One pint of alcohol, half-ounce of ammonia, four ounces of Spanish whiting, half pint of rain water. Apply with a sponge and wipe with a soft cloth.—*Mrs. Elbridge Wood.*

CAMPHOR ICE.

Equal parts of gum camphor, white wax, spermaceti and sweet oil, melted together, and stirred constantly until cold.

COLOGNE WATER.

Six drachms each of oil of lavender, oil of burgamot, and essence of lemon, one drachm of oil of rosemary, twenty drops of oil of cinnamon, three quarts of alcohol.—*Miss Caroline Duncan.*

LIME WATER.

Put a lump of fresh, unslacked lime, about as large as a half peck measure into an unpainted pail. Pour over slowly, so as not to slack too fast, about four gallons of hot water, and stir thoroughly. Let it settle, and stir again two or three times in twenty-four hours. Then bottle all that can be poured off clear.

A little of it may be taken for acidity of the stomach. A teaspoonful in a cup of milk will make it digestible when otherwise it might not be.

The lime water is also very useful for cleansing small milk vessels, nursing bottles, &c.

BRINE FOR BUTTER.

Dissolve a cup of coarse salt in two quarts of water, just boil, skim and set away to cool. Pour over the butter when cold.

PICKLE FOR EGGS.

One gallon of water, one pound of quick-lime, one-half pint of salt, one ounce, (or a quarter of a cup,) of cream of tartar.—*Mrs. C. W. Train.*

WEIGHTS AND MEASURES.

One quart of sifted flour is one pound.
One pint of granulated sugar is a pound.
Two cups of butter, packed, are a pound.
Ten eggs are a pound.
Five cups of sifted flour are a pound.
Eight even tablespoonfuls are a gill.

Broth will be more nutritious if thickened in part with tapioca, rather than wholly with rice.

Add one-quarter of a cup of boiling water to any rule for sponge cake, to make it roll easily for jelly-cake.

Sausages, liver, shad and many other breakfast dishes which are usually cooked in the spider or on a griddle, are equally nice cooked by the hot morning fire in the oven, thus avoiding much smoke and unpleasant odor in the kitchen.

Two tablespoonfuls of newly-fallen snow, stirred in quickly and baked immediately, are equal to one egg in puddings or pancakes.

Raised bread is very good baked on the griddle for breakfast, when there is not time to rise it in pans. Roll about half as thick as for biscuit, cut round, and have the griddle moderately hot.

If in cooking you have used too much sugar, a little salt will correct the error; if too much salt, correct with sugar.

Morning's milk, says a German philosopher, commonly yields more cream than the evening's, at the same temperature.

To prevent contagion from eruptive disease, keep constantly in the sick room plates of sliced raw onions. As fast as they become discolored, replace with fresh ones.

For a cold, pare off the yellow rind of a lemon and slice the remainder. Put layers of lemon and sugar in a deep plate, cover close with a saucer, and set in a warm place. Use freely.

A poultice of soda water and flour will cure the sting of a wasp, slices of raw onion the sting of a bee.

For chilblains, apply iodine once or twice a day, as the skin will allow.

To restore from stroke of lightning, shower with cold water.

For a burn, apply poultices of grated raw potato, every few minutes; or, use common bread soda; or, a wash of linseed oil and lime water, half and half.

Keep coffee in a glass fruit can, and screw on the cover tight. Keep tea in a tin canister.

To strengthen a new earthen teapot, potter's ware vessel, or iron kettle, fill with cold water and heat very gradually indeed to the boiling point.

An excellent disinfectant is made by dissolving half a pound of copperas in two gallons of water.

When fruit burns on the bottom of a porcelain kettle, put in a tablespoonful of soda and some boiling water and let it remain a few minutes.

To loosen a glass stopper, pour around it a little sweet oil, close to the mouth of the bottle, and lay it near the fire; afterward wrap a thick cloth round the end of a stick and strike the stopper gently.

The hands and nails are kept clean and white, soft and supple, by daily use of lemon instead of soap.

To clean tinted paint, use nice whiting instead of soap. Wet a piece of flannel in clean, warm water, squeeze nearly dry, dip into the whiting and with it rub the soiled paint; afterwards wash in clean water and rub dry with a soft chamois.

To renew velvet, heat an iron moderately hot, cover it with a wet cloth and hold it under the velvet on the wrong side. The steam will penetrate the velvet, and the pile can be raised with a common clothes brush.

White spots can be removed from crape by the use of clear alcohol.

The squeaking of boots may be prevented by driving a few pegs in the middle of the sole.

Cranberries may be kept all winter by placing them in a firkin of water, in the cellar.

Embroidery, to be ironed nicely, should be put upon flannel and ironed until dry.

Spots on zinc may be removed by the use of kerosene.

Nickle plate may be polished with pulverized borax. Use with it hot water and a little soap; rub dry with Canton flannel.

Tin ware should be washed in hot soft water. Soap the cloth well, and rub the tin briskly; pour boiling water over it and wipe dry.

When ribbons or silk are laid aside they should be wrapped or folded in coarse brown paper, which, as it contains a portion of tar and turpentine, will preserve the color of the silk and prevent white silk from turning yellow. White paper should *never* be used.

Silver ware is often tarnished in houses where hard coal is used. This tarnish can be entirely prevented by painting the silver with a soft brush dipped into alcohol in which some collodion has been dissolved. The liquid dries immediately and forms a thin, invisible coating upon the silver, which protects it from all effects of the atmosphere, etc. It can be removed at any time by dipping the article in hot water.

A silver spoon put into a tumbler or glass jar will prevent its breaking when filled with hot water.

Clean oil-cloths with milk and water; a brush and soap will ruin them.

All kinds of tubs and firkins should be turned upside down on the cellar floor to prevent their leaking.

Use one tablespoonful Paris green in a pailful of water, to kill canker worms. Apply with a large syringe. Good for all insects that infest shrubbery.

To cleanse marble, use two ounces of common soda, one of pumice stone, one of finely powdered chalk. Sift them through a fine sieve and mix with water. Rub the mixture well over the marble. Then wash with soap and water.

To clean hair brushes, wash in spirits of ammonia and hot water, and dry with a coarse towel.

To remove tar, rub well with lard, then wash with soap and warm water.

Scatter sprigs of wormwood in places infested with black ants.

The little red ants will leave closets where sea-sand is sprinkled, or where oyster shells are laid.

A valued majolica pitcher was accidentally cracked, and thus rendered of no use beyond ornament. It was put into a pail of skimmed milk and boiled for some time, the crack closed, and the pitcher has again become a useful member of society.

A hot vessel set upon varnished furniture will leave a white spot. Such a spot can be removed by wetting a bit of flannel in alcohol and rubbing briskly over the place until the spot is effaced; then wet another flannel in linseed oil and rub over lightly.

To remove oil from a carpet or any woolen stuff, apply buckwheat plentifully. Never use water, or liquid of any kind.

Indian meal, moistened and applied to soiled places on carpets, will often remove all traces of the spots, and without the slightest injury to the most delicate colors.

A paste made from common starch and cold water will remove stains from mattresses. If the first application is not sufficient to do it thoroughly, repeat, but the first paste must remain for many hours before the second is applied.

Cover pickle jars with grape leaves, changing them occasionally. They exclude the air, and impart a delightful flavor to the pickles.

TABLE OF CONTENTS.

	PAGE.
SOUPS,	7
FISH,	12
MEATS.	18
FRAGMENTS.	27
EGGS,	31
SAUCES AND SALADS.	34
VEGETABLES.	39
BREAD,	45
BREAKFAST AND TEA.	52
PIES,	62
PUDDINGS.	68
DESSERTS.	81
CAKES.	89
PRESERVES.	108
PICKLES,	114
CANDIES.	118
BEVERAGES.	121
FOR THE SICK.	124
LAUNDRY,	128
MISCELLANEOUS,	131

AN UNBROKEN RECORD OF SUCCESS

DURYEAS' Glen Cove Manufacturing Co. received the ONLY GOLD MEDAL, over all Competitors, at PARIS EXPOSITION, 1878.

DURYEAS' + SATIN + GLOSS + STARCH,

Gives a Beautiful, White, Glossy and Lasting Finish.

NO OTHER STARCH SO EASILY USED OR SO ECONOMICAL.

DURYEAS' IMPROVED CORN STARCH

FROM THE BEST SELECTED INDIAN CORN,

Warranted Perfectly Pure.

DURYEAS' STARCH,

IN EVERY INSTANCE OF COMPETITION HAS RECEIVED THE —HIGHEST—AWARD.—

In addition to Medals, many Diplomas have been received. The following are a few of the characterizing terms of award: at—

LONDON, 1862, for quality,	"EXCEEDINGLY EXCELLENT."
PARIS, 1867, "	"PERFECTION OF PREPARATION."
PARIS, 1878, "	"BEST PRODUCTION OF ITS KIND."
CENTENNIAL, 1876, for	"NOTABLE OR ABSOLUTE PURITY."
BRUSSELS, 1876, for	"REMARKABLE EXCELLENCE."
FRANKLIN INST., PENN.,	"FOR SUPERIOR MERIT, NOT ALONE AS BEING

THE BEST OF THE KIND EXHIBITED, BUT AS THE BEST KNOWN TO EXIST IN THE MARKET OF AMERICAN PRODUCTIONS."

FOR SALE BY GROCERS GENERALLY.

Emerson's Bazaar

ALWAYS IN STOCK, A LARGE VARIETY AND THE LATEST IMPROVEMENTS IN

KITCHEN FURNISHING GOODS

IMPROVED BREAD MIXER.

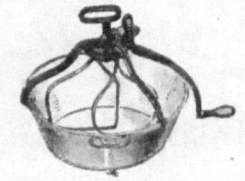

By its use, dough is thoroughly kneaded, and much hard labor avoided.

VEGETABLE BOILER.

All sizes. Used for boiling vegetables and eggs.

COCOA POTS.

Sizes from 1 pt. to 3 qts.; best of tin.

DOVER EGG-BEATER.

The best known.

CAKE BOXES AND CHESTS

Made of tin, finely japanned, either in box form, or in upright chests.

JELLY MOULDS.

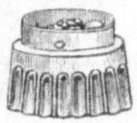

Seamless molds, of any desired size, for jelly, blanc mange, etc.

GEM SIFTER.

Holds exactly 1 qt. For sifting flour, meal, etc.

SPICE BOXES.

By their use, spices retain their original strength.

FARINA BOILER.

A variety of sizes. Indispensable for making blanc mange, cooking oatmeal, etc., etc.

TIN COLANDER.

For washing or steaming purposes.

PUDDING BOILER.

For steaming pudding and bread.

SQUASH STRAINER.

Made of first-class tin, and very desirable.

MERRIMACK ST., THIRTY-FIVE & THIRTY-SEVEN,
Haverhill, - - - - Mass.

G. E. CURTIS & Co.,

—— MANUFACTURERS AND JOBBERS OF ——

PICKLES,
PRESERVES,

KETCHUPS, HORSE RADISH, MUSTARDS, SAUCES,

Jams, Jellies, Olives, Etc.,

White Wine and Cider Vinegar.

WEST NEPTUNE ST., LYNN, MASS.

FINE FLAVORING EXTRACTS AND SPICES.

Success in Fine Cooking can only be attained by the use of Pure and Nice Flavoring Extracts and Spices.

Understanding This, I Manufacture a Line of Extra Nice

UNADULTERATED EXTRACTS.

INTENDED EXPRESSLY FOR FINE COOKING, Viz:

ALMOND, LEMON, ORANGE,
ROSE, VANILLA, WINTERGREEN.

My EXTRACT VANILLA is one of the specialties of my establishment, made from the Best Quality of VANILLA BEAN, and free from any adulteration whatever. My Spices are of the Best Quality, and warranted STRICTLY PURE. The List includes—

Cassia, Cloves, Pimento, Ginger, Mace, &c., &c.

CHAS. B. EMERSON, The Druggist.

2 Merrimack, 1 & 3 Bridge Sts., - - Haverhill, Mass.

PROPRIETOR OF EMERSON'S GOLDENSEAL.

For DYSPEPSIA, DIABETES, *GLUTEN*
LUNG TROUBLES, NERVOUS DEBILITY.

New Waste-Repairing Bread and Gem Flour,

FREE FROM BRAN OR STARCH

IT IS A BRAIN, NERVE, BONE AND MUSCLE-BUILDING FLOUR, CONTAINING TO THE FULLEST EXTENT THE LIFE-GIVING AND NUTRITIVE ELEMENTS OF TWO KINDS OF THE BEST WHEAT.

ADAPTED TO FAMILY USE.

FLOUR

SEND FOR CIRCULAR.
FARWELL & RHINES, Prop's
WATERTOWN, N. Y.

JAMES PYLE'S PEARLINE

EVERY LADY
Married or Single,
Housekeeping or Not,
SHOULD BE ACQUAINTED WITH THE UTILITY OF

PYLE'S PEARLINE,

For washing small articles in a basin, cleaning jewelry, hair, combs or brushes, removing stains or ink spots, and for dish-washing, as well as for beautifying linens. For the bath it is luxurious and healthful. It takes the place of soap, is entirely harmless, is universally approved, and its value is apparent on trial.

Sold by all Grocers, but beware of Vile Imitations.

——MANUFACTURED ONLY BY——

JAMES PYLE, - - NEW YORK.

IRA K. MESSER,
41 MAIN STREET, - HAVERHILL, MASS.

Fine Groceries

Of Every Description.

Superior Teas and Coffees, Pure Spices, Condiments, Sauces, Onions, Pickles, Limes, Jellies, Imported and American Preserves in Plain and Fancy Jars, Fresh Fruits in their Season.

CREAM OF TARTAR.

The Subscriber would respectfully announce to the students of this valuable work that he pays particular attention to the selection of the above-named article, as well as of the

BEST AND PUREST BREAD SODA,

That can be procured. Every lot that is received is subjected to a thorough chemical test that proves its purity beyond a doubt. Hundreds of the best cooks in this city and vicinity are constantly testifying to its superiority over the ordinary article of commerce.

THOMAS H. BAILEY, Apothecary.
No. 23 Merrimack Street, - - Haverhill, Mass.

M. L. STOVER,
——WHOLESALE AND RETAIL DEALER IN——

Meats and Provisions

VEAL ALL THE YEAR ROUND,

GAME OF ALL KINDS FURNISHED TO ORDER

Fresh Fruits and Berries in their Season, a Specialty.

14 EMERSON ST., HAVERHILL, MASS.

www.ingramcontent.com/pod-product-compliance
Lightning Source LLC
Chambersburg PA
CBHW030359170426
43202CB00010B/1426